THE MARRIAGE DIALOGUE

THE MARRIAGE DIALOGUE

A. Lynn Scoresby

Brigham Young University

ADDISON-WESLEY PUBLISHING COMPANY

Reading, Massachusetts · Menlo Park, California
London · Amsterdam · Don Mills, Ontario · Sydney

This book is in the
ADDISON-WESLEY SERIES IN SOCIOLOGY

ISBN 0-201-06789-7
ABCDEFGHIJ-AL-7987

To Dorothy, my dialogue partner

PREFACE

Couples entering into marriage today are faced with a paradox—because of the rising divorce rate, they believe that failure in marriage is more probable, and so they tend to reduce their commitment or investment, in hopes of avoiding the pain that would result if theirs should fail. Unfortunately, the very fact of joining in a marital contract with low commitment lays the foundation for the failure. We often live alone or unfulfilled, thinking we are justified in our limited investment, whereas if we entered into marriage with increased commitment, our chances for happiness would be greatly improved.

Good marriages are most frequently achieved by the sustained effort of two committed people. With some effort we can usually acquire the skills enabling us to find satisfaction. The more skill or success we acquire, the easier it is to invest, and the continuation of this positive cycle can be used to realize the rich potential marriage has to offer.

This book is written to describe marital communication skills. When applied correctly they will prove well worth the effort required to learn them. But learning to communicate effectively and fully with another person is not an easy nor simple task. The elements of a continued dialogue are varied and complex. And failure to communicate is not—as some might think—a minor difficulty. This inadequacy both reflects and contributes to a host of conflicts and problems. Consequently, couples who take the time and effort to be successful communicators contribute a great deal to their own success in marriage.

In writing this book, my intent is to affirm that marriage can be a place of happiness, and to deny that it is an unlikely arrangement for our modern day. I suggest, in fact, that we have not yet learned all there is to know about it, and that we would be mistaken to look to other forms of male-female living as offering more potential. Instead, I believe we will benefit if we renew our study of marriage communication, if we better prepare ourselves, and if we develop increased confidence that our own marriage can and will succeed. Some of the communication skills that are needed can be learned prior to marriage. The rest, fortunately, we can learn while we live our lives as two people in a fascinating and continual dialogue of working, talking, playing, and loving in one way or another.

Provo, Utah   A. L. S.
January 1977

CONTENTS

CHAPTER
1
THE ROLE OF COMMUNICATION IN MARRIAGE

Before getting married a man and woman usually wonder whether or not they will be successful. Some couples indulge in lengthy analytic discussions, and others consult friends and relatives in attempts to create confidence their marriage will succeed. Often, however, even the best investigation falls short of providing definite answers. What in fact makes a successful marriage? Most behavioral scientists are beginning to believe that the answer to this question lies in the way a couple communicate with each other.

Watzlawick et al. (1967) wrote that in marriage it is not possible to *not* communicate because all behavior, including words and actions, can convey meaning. It seems that in successful marriages, as compared with less successful ones, actions performed or statements made in intramarital exchanges have the same meaning for both. Meyer Katz (1964), for example, found that marital satisfaction was closely related to whether the words used by each person had the same emotional meaning for both—that is, whether the emotions of the person sending the message evoked similar emotions within the receiver. Good communication, in this sense, does not seem to depend on *what* people talk about; it is *how* they do it that makes the difference.

There is a lot of truth in the idea that marrying an individual is like marrying his or her family. Impressions and values that are rooted in the profound and intense relationships of early childhood shape the meaning of messages sent and received later in marriage. The communication style eventually emerging in a marriage is a combination of the styles of two families, the husband's and the wife's. This idea has been supported in the writings of Tharp (1963), who reported that when a husband's concept of his father and of himself as a man matches the wife's concept of a father and a man, there is an increased possibility that the two will communicate more effectively about the husband's role as a man and as a father. He found that this matching is related to high marital satisfaction. The more similarly two people view their families, the greater the probability they will succeed in their own marital communication.

Many of us are not fortunate enough to enter a marriage with someone who has exactly the same or even quite similar background. Even so, most of us communicate well in some areas but not in others. Generally, when communication seems to be poor, it is because rather than clearing up a small difference we let strong feelings develop which also are not discussed. In subsequent attempts to communicate about the difference, the strong feelings reappear, making it gradually more and more difficult for a sender to express what is really meant and a hearer to accurately receive. This difficulty can then spread from a small area of difference to several, eventually affecting or engulfing a large portion of the total marriage.

Fortunately, two people can give a positive impetus to their marriage as easily as they can let it slip into an unsatisfactory state. If good communication is the key to marital success, then it seems desirable for a couple to learn to employ useful methods rather than leave the quality of their relationship to chance life events. Instead of hoping that good fortune comes and no ill winds blow their way, a couple can actively work on effective communication techniques and lay their own solid marital foundation. All that is required is to learn what techniques can be successful and then use them. Not that this is always easy to do—getting good communication in marriage is often a difficult and complex task requiring a good deal of concentrated effort. But, as people who are happily married can attest, it is worth working together to achieve accurate communication.

Probably the first step in creating positive marital communication is for a couple to recognize that their relationship encompasses everything each sees, feels, or hears from the other. All is shared. While the marriage lasts, it is not possible to communicate nothing. When together as man and woman we participate in a special dialogue of words, feelings, and actions. It may be eloquent. It is always profound.

Once both people fully comprehend the idea that all marital events are shared, even those that seem individual and unique, it is less likely that either will pretend that one of them can be isolated, separated, or protected from the other. Instead our energies can be turned toward participation in the dialogue of marriage, making it our chief reward and source of fulfillment. When both come to it with this attitude a relationship holds the promise of excitement, challenge, and great learning.

THE MEANING OF THE MARRIAGE CONTEXT

The second step in creating positive communication is to recognize that among all the possible types of relationships, marriage is unique. There is no other association like it and—because communication is greatly influenced by the setting or *context* in which it occurs—the communication within that relationship is unique as well.

A context is made up of a time, a place, and the people who perform certain roles and who have a purpose or reason for being together. In the context of marriage, words and actions may mean something different than identical words and actions between two people in another two-person association. Suppose, for example, that a man criticizes his secretary for work poorly done. The employer-employee relationship may dictate that she respond submissively to his criticism. But if, on the same day, the man as a husband criticizes his wife for work poorly done, the husband-wife context may dictate to the wife that she be critical in return. Many people who find a given behavior successful in one context try to apply the same behavior in marriage, only to find failure instead. In effect, the total context of marriage largely defines how words and actions of husband and wife are interpreted.

We have stressed that the marriage context is unique. What characteristics make it so? One is *the belief that the relationship is going to last a long time, presumably forever.* Events in the present cannot as easily be ignored and must be responded to because they are quite likely to affect the future. Thus little acts that are passed over in other contexts are more likely to be noticed. Repeated disturbances are less easily tolerated because they likewise may have long-term repercussions. Furthermore, often what a husband or wife says in ordinary conversation may be analyzed for meanings and motivations far beyond their original intent.

The belief that a relationship will last indefinitely influences the order of priority assigned to maintenance of the marriage, although not in the same way for all couples. Young married couples attending school, for instance, often skimp on the efforts needed to maintain their marriage, thinking they will give it greater attention when school is completed. Some sadly learn, when that time comes, that they have no marriage left to maintain, or that their problems have grown to such attention-demanding proportions that the maintenance aspect is forgotten. Other couples view the likely permanence of the marital commitment as an added pressure. They feel a great burden and stress as they "work hard" to make their marriage a good one. Sometimes this devotion is overdone, and the resulting lack of enjoyment and fun kill the marriage they are working so hard to perpetuate.

On the other hand, knowing and hoping that marriage can last forever produces positive effects as well as negative ones. It can, for example, add confidence, trust, and stability. When we fully accept the idea of a perpetuating relationship, we can determine more successfully whether we will allow it to affect us positively or negatively. Any couple could benefit by examining how each partner handles the fact that their relationship may last forever.

A second unique feature of the marriage context is that each person has *high expectations for achieving understanding and intimacy* in the relationship. This includes not only sexual involvement, but also the intimacy of knowing more about each other's feelings than does anyone else. Ordinarily, when one expects to be known by another, he or she anticipates being understood. Thus in marriage, more so than in other relationships, great importance is attached to the ability to understand. It is not uncommon that a husband or wife becomes frustrated because a partner has not correctly interpreted feelings or is not being sufficiently sensitive. Even without a forthright statement of what is needed and how one feels, the partner is somehow supposed to accurately sense and satisfy the other's "needs." This expectation of understanding is often a yardstick by which a person judges the amount of love felt by a partner. If one is understood by a spouse, then it is credited to that person's love and consideration. If one is not understood, there are doubts about being loved as well.

The expectation of understanding naturally influences communication within the context of marriage. For example, a spouse may believe that something need be said only once, even somewhat vaguely, and the partner should triumphantly distill the true meaning of the message. Expecting that marriage partners will always understand each other, such a person is lulled into thinking he or she does not need to speak clearly nor attempt to listen carefully. But instead of expecting understanding to be easy and natural, we should recognize that it must be worked at and learned. The existence of understanding is a vital ingredient in marriage and is in fact a purpose of marital talking, so let us treat the need to understand with the importance it deserves.

A third way in which marriage is unique is that the partners must engage in *tasks that simultaneously and intensely involve both people.* Survival and economic concerns, the conceiving and rearing of children, the satisfaction of sexual needs, the affirmation of religious values, and the pursuit of social relations with other people involve both the man and the woman. And because each bears a share of these mutual tasks, each feels compelled to communicate with the other about them. Ignoring messages about them—or failing to send any—can be viewed as indifference, a high marital crime.

While each partner may contribute individually to the accomplishment of marital tasks, it is seldom acceptable for one to be much more involved than the other. The overinvolvement of one, such as in child rearing, may preclude similar participation of the other—who can then be criticized for not getting involved! In fact, the requirement of joint task accomplishment provides a way for husband and wife to assess each other's level of involvement.

Much communication in marriage is about how each performs tasks and how well the tasks are accomplished. In fact, the topics the two people talk about are largely determined by these joint tasks. And, since the tasks are by their nature laden with importance for each person, communicating about them is made similarly important.

Another unique characteristic of the marriage context is the *role given it by our culture.* Because society expects married people to perform cooperatively, it affords great protection to the relationship—and imposes great responsibility on it—by means of legal sanctions, social pressure, and moral constraints. Much of the time married people perform successfully the roles our culture prescribes. But sometimes the external societal constraints make a husband and wife feel they are staying together out of obligation rather than by choice. The issue of "having to" versus "wanting to" can drastically affect marital communication: messages from a person who "wants" to be involved usually mean something different to the perceptive receiver than do messages from someone who seems to "have to" be a part of things. Frequently each partner may listen and watch to see if his or her communication is sincerely and authentically joined by the other person more than occasionally, for this seems to be another indicator of the spouse's level of commitment. Ironically, when this concern becomes too important, the one who worries about the other is likely to communicate mistrust. The partner then interprets mistrust as lack of commitment, and thus a cycle of suspicion is created. Eventually, neither has much motivation to be a part of the relationship.

Finally, marriage is unique because it is a relationship that may be entered into with *differing motivations*. These differences may relate to how the two people view their sex roles or to their family and cultural backgrounds. Frequently, the reasons that women marry are somewhat different from those of men. In any case, since husband and wife may not want the same things from marriage, their dialogue has to be flexible enough to provide for the needs of both.

The long-term nature of the marriage commitment, the expectations of finding understanding, the requirement of accomplishing joint tasks, the role defined by our culture, different reasons for marrying and staying married—all make marriage a context different from any other. And because it is different, requirements for communication between people within it will differ accordingly. If it is true that good communication can lead to happier marriages, then ways need to be found that will allow a couple to send and receive messages with accuracy and clarity. Furthermore, these methods must take account of the factors that make marriage unique. The types of communication and the communication techniques described in this book are those most appropriate to the marriage context, and we therefore shall refer to them collectively as the marriage dialogue.

ASPECTS OF THE MARRIAGE DIALOGUE

In this book we consider nine areas of communication that are part of the marriage dialogue. Each has a purpose and satisfies in some way the unique demands that marriage makes on a man and a woman.

The expectation that the marriage will perpetuate itself can be successfully managed when each person is aware of the purpose behind the messages a partner sends. That is, if each can hear both the words and the intention behind them, the partners will communicate more clearly. And when messages are accurately sent and received each person can become more fully involved and enjoy the marriage as it is lived, rather than being unduly distracted by the future.

Because men and women expect marriage to bring understanding, they need to learn the language of intimacy. This form of communication satisfies the emotional needs of each person to be known and affirmed by the other. Among the important marital tasks that are determined in part by our culture, one is the meeting of sexual needs, and so a couple's communication about their sexual relationship is of great importance. The performance of other tasks requires making decisions and negotiating. Furthermore, since the two people are individuals from different backgrounds and with different needs, it will help if their communication skills include ways to solve problems, manage conflict, and make their relationship sufficiently flexible to incorporate both personalities. Finally, the marriage relationship requires that the couple develop a variety of ways of expressing their love for each other.

Interpreting Marital Messages

The human brain has the capacity to simultaneously hear what people say and analyze why they are saying it. If this is done every time someone speaks, conversation will become increasingly frustrating. But over time, a certain amount of such analysis permits us to develop guesses and hypotheses about why people are saying something. Usually, once this happens, we are responsive as much to what we think is their intention as we are to their words. Thus the words a married person speaks tend to become the vehicle for an underlying message. This message is the guess we made about the intentions of the person speaking. Then, having collected several bits and pieces of such information, we sift them and place them into some categories which are eventually used to create a general style of relating.

What if our guesses about someone's intentions are incorrect? Will our interpretations of their messages be also? Very likely so, and for this reason it is useful for marriage partners to develop skill in correctly interpreting each other's intentions. Chapter 2, which deals with interpreting messages, explores some common intentions underlying people's communication and then explains how these contribute to the formation of relationship styles.

The Language of Understanding and Intimacy

Almost all of us hope that in marriage we will be understood— that someone will know about our feelings, the way we think and what we value. Being understood leads to a sense of security, giving comfort and peace of mind. A couple who share their feelings develop a sense of mutual inclusion which satisfies a profound need, the need to belong to someone somewhere. Martin Buber, writing of understanding and intimacy, suggested that:

> Men need, and it is granted to them, to confirm one another in their individual being by means of genuine meetings. But beyond this they need, and it is granted to them, to see the truth, which the soul gains by its struggle, light up to the other . . . and even so be confirmed. (*Knowledge of Man*, p. 69)

The language of understanding and intimacy helps each partner confirm the worth and identity of the other. In Chapter 3, the style of communication and the procedures for achieving understanding and intimacy are discussed.

Sexual Communication

The desire for sexual gratification exerts a powerful influence upon human beings. In addition to affording a physical outlet, however, the sexual relationship in marriage can afford the man and woman a unification and blending of two otherwise separate personalities. At its best, marital sex is a cooperative, fully and freely given expression of erotic and emotional fulfillment.

Husband and wife in this association have a primary responsibility for their own sexual experience and a secondary, but important, responsibility for the satisfaction of their partner. When sexual activity is seen as a duty for a wife and a demand from a husband, or vice versa, it can mean dissatisfaction for both. In fact, unresolved attitudes and physical-emotional differences can become so discomforting that sexual expression is limited and controlled, failing to reach its full potential. Achieving good sexual expression is a major step toward a successful marital dialogue and, for most couples, it is possible if they learn to communicate successfully.

Making Decisions

Each person before marriage may have learned to make decisions when alone, but the cooperative decision-making required in marriage may be foreign to both. Making quality decisions, however, is one key to accomplishing the joint tasks of marriage to the satisfaction of both partners. Cooperating in decision-making helps enhance this sense of being committed to one another, and eventually the time devoted to making good decisions will increase total productivity, allowing more of the necessary tasks to be completed. Fortunately, a good procedure for decision-making can be learned, and a couple who become proficient at it will go far in their attempts to achieve a happy marriage.

Negotiating

Making decisions is one thing, implementing them is another. Almost every married couple has had the experience of making a decision that appeared to be reasonable, but was never implemented. Marital negotiation increases the probability that a couple will act upon their decisions. Like decision-making, negotiation communicates commitment; but in addition it communicates a reciprocity of *action*. Negotiation draws each person into active participation.

The consequences of an unwillingness to act can be harmful. Viewing what appears to be indifference on the part of a spouse, a marriage partner may attempt to maneuver the spouse into increased involvement. Nagging, criticism, blaming, accusing, and lengthy lectures are common methods of doing this. However, this behavior usually places the hearer in the position of being more involved only at the price of conceding that his or her partner has more power. Thus, even if a person does become more involved after being nagged or criticized, he or she may seek ways of denying that the other person has gained increased control. And since this usually takes the form of refusing to comply with further requests, a painful standoff results. Learning to negotiate is a way for two people to directly and positively influence the extent of each other's involvement in a task requiring mutual cooperation.

Time Driving

Observant couples find that many events in their dialogue of marriage follow a sequential pattern. For example, a husband's actions elicit some negative response by his wife, which in turn provokes a certain reaction on the part of the husband, and so forth. Most couples have created several such sequences which they invariably play out to a painful conclusion, and the sequences tend to occur regularly. A readily identifiable sequence might be labeled "arguing about who was supposed to pay the bills," or "you don't love me." Because each sequence is marked by a definite series of interpersonal behaviors, a couple can identify these, analyze the meaning of each behavior, and change the way they will view each other's behavior in the future. This process, called time driving, makes a couple more aware of the meaning of each other's actions when a bad sequence seems to be developing. By mutual agreement, they can agree to eliminate the sequence, and this helps them develop a sense of control over events they experience together.

Metacommunication

Marital communication, like other interaction, occurs at two levels. One level, the "report" aspect, is carried in the meanings of the words themselves. The second, or "command" aspect of communication, tells people what to do with what they hear. When a person uses sarcasm, for example, the spoken words by themselves may mean something positive, but the voice tone, hand movements, and other nonverbal behavior tell or "command" a listener to interpret the message oppositely.

When we are in a continuing relationship, we act in myriads of complex ways toward each other. Our words report what each wishes to communicate, and some actions command what to do with the words. As part of the marriage dialogue, metacommunication permits a couple to talk about *how* they communicate. The prefix *meta* means "about," so *metacommunication* means communicating about communication. Couples who approach metacommunication as prescribed in Chapter 8 will be able to make their relationship flexible and changing. This helps reduce the feeling that nothing can be changed and improved.

Managing Conflict

Two people bound together and requiring close communication will inevitably experience periods of tension, anger, or anxiety. Often this produces marital conflict, which both wish to resolve without harming the relationship. To do this, they need to view marital conflict as a prelude to behavior change. With this interpretation, a couple can bring about the desired change in themselves and their relationship without suffering feelings of personal inadequacy or the threat of a dissolving marriage. Conflict, when it is managed wisely, can be a healthy and natural part of a continuing two-person relationship. With adequate management skills a couple can face their problems with confidence.

What Love Is

The most profound communication of love in a marital dialogue is not through the words "I love you" or through gifts bestowed on a partner. While these are helpful, they are less significant than a gentle response to angry words, a confident expectation of trust, and the active assumption of being loved. There are those who contend that in happy marriages the emotion of love is not essential as long as there is effective communication. Nevertheless, there are things shared between a man and woman that defy explanation, and though unspoken-of, their presence is known. These events are the true symbols of love and can be made part of each marriage.

CHAPTER 2
INTERPRETING MARITAL MESSAGES

Although most married people hope to have good communication, many do not know exactly what it is nor how to achieve it. Good communication is probably best defined as the accurate sending and receiving of information. It occurs only when a message sent by one person is interpreted by the receiver in the way the sender intends. This means that both the sending and the receiving of a message must be effective.

Quite often, we try to achieve good communication by polishing our ability to send. We take formal training through speech, drama, or debate courses. Or we use informal methods of trying to say "exactly what we mean." We do recognize, then, that poor communication may be caused by the inadequacy of the sender, and the emphasis we give to saying what we really mean suggests how much we want to be understood.

Too often, however, we neglect to develop the skills of listening successfully—in other words, we don't know how to be accurate receivers. Obviously this problem creates the possibility of poor communication. The unique context of marriage requires that a receiver not only listen to the words, but correctly interpret the intention behind the spoken message. Neither aspect of the receiving process can be ignored if a couple wish to be accurate communicators.

Our reasons for communicating are shaped by our expectations. We believe we need or can get certain things from certain people, and we then try, by communication, to get those things from the specific people who share the context or relationship at a certain time. To have accurate communication, a husband and wife need to know what each wants to obtain. Then both can interpret each other's messages in light of these expectations.

What do people expect to get from marriage? Do all of us have similar expectations? Or does every individual hope for some fairly unique things? This chapter is aimed at supplying some answers to these questions. Keep in mind, however, that the context of marriage is unique in part because we believe we can get some things from it that we cannot obtain in other relationships. Furthermore, although the marital relationship is a dynamic, evolving, and ongoing dialogue, there is not an infinite number of ways husbands and wives communicate. Two people talk, act, listen, and interpret in some fairly definite patterns. Collectively, these patterns form an interaction style that tends to be regular, in the same situations, over time. Once formed, it is this style of interaction that shapes how one person perceives the other.

That is, through the interaction itself, a wife and husband gather bits of information about each other's personality. A cycle is formed consisting of (a) a style of communication leading to (b) a view of each other's personality which leads to (c) a perpetuation of the communication style. To achieve good communication, a receiver must not only be able to correctly interpret the sender's purpose for communicating, but also be aware of the way the couple's style of interaction shapes how each is perceived by the other.

THE PURPOSE OF MARITAL MESSAGES

We have stated that the reason for sending a given message depends on what one can expect to get from another person, in the relationship, at a given time. What possibilities then does marriage afford a man and woman? And will knowing these enable a couple to more accurately recognize the intention underlying a specific message? This section attempts to provide answers to both of these questions.

While every marriage has its specific and different possibilities, some objectives of marital communication seem to be nearly universal. One way of describing these is provided by Kantor and Lehr (1975). They write about the objectives of communication in terms of three broad focal areas which they call *target dimensions*. In marriage (or in any intense family relationship) people are likely to spend more time communicating along these three dimensions than they do in other situations. The first dimension is *affect*, or the sharing of emotional experience. More specifically, people wish to achieve a feeling of intimacy, of love and nurturance. A second dimension is *power*. Each partner wishes to have a say in the management of marital tasks—what gets done, when it gets done, and who does it. This type of communication is therefore concerned with each person's freedom, or lack of it, and with how restraints are exerted. The third target dimension is *meaning*. Husbands and wives look to each other for help in clarifying or affirming their own ideas, moral values, or world views.

When a husband and wife send messages to each other it is quite likely they intend to obtain something related to power, affect, or meaning. The partner who is the receiver of information responds as much to the perceived intent of the message as to the literal content of it. If the receiver does not correctly identify the purpose of a message, accurate communication will not result and appropriate responses will not be given. Suppose, for instance, that a sender intends to obtain affection (affect) but gives an unclear request, one that is interpreted as seeking power. The receiver will, of course, respond as though the request were for power, affection will not be given, and the sender will feel frustrated and misunderstood. This kind of miscommunication is illustrated in the following example.

The Johnsons had been married for five years. Bill had been reared in a family who frequently did things to show affection

*and care for one another. While this was also true for Helen,
she was an only child. She had lived with parents who were
patient, calm, and considerate. When Bill and Helen had
two small children, Helen was not as able to get the housework done and Bill began to make comments about the "dirty
bathroom" or "disorganized kitchen." Finally one day Bill
angrily said, "Do I have to get mad to get you to do something I want?" Offended, Helen asked why he felt that way.
He replied by saying that a dirty house bothered him and
"even though you know I don't like it, you won't do anything about it. You don't care about anything I want."
Helen's response was a surprise. "I don't do what you ask
because I don't want you telling me what to do or when to
do it."*

In this example, Bill was looking for evidence of affection by
asking his wife to clean the home for him. Instead of seeing his
intention, Helen viewed his behavior as an attempt to obtain power
and responded by not complying.

Clearly, marital satisfaction depends in some part on whether
a receiver can, in most cases, correctly recognize the purpose behind a message. If misunderstanding of intent repeatedly occurs, it
is difficult for couples to feel happy or fulfilled. Thus both husband
and wife can benefit from knowing how to recognize requests for
affect, power, and meaning.

Affect

Each person has unique ways of seeking the experience of shared
affect, and any couple can benefit from exploring the differences
in their affect-seeking messages. Beyond this, however, most of us
use some similar methods, and knowing these will prove useful.

As a rule, people seek the type of affect that is loving, warm,
and intimate. Usually this can be obtained by sending one's own
messages of love, warmth, and intimacy, not only by direct verbal
expression, but also by touching, by disclosing one's strong inner
feelings, and by showing interest and attention toward another
person. Such efforts toward gaining positive affect are usually well

understood. But others that are frequently exhibited are less easy to recognize. Consider, for example, expressions of boredom, tiredness, crankiness with children, low levels of productivity, or feigned illness. These are often intended to elicit evidence of affectionate concern. The same is true of self-criticism, exaggerated attempts to win approval, and self-isolation. All of these at one time or another can be used by a sender to request and obtain positive affect in marriage.

It should be emphasized that the central purpose of this particular type of marital message is the *sharing* of affect. If a husband and wife find it difficult or impossible to share positive affect, they may resort to communicating about negative things as a substitute. This possibility is examined by Bach and Wyden (1968), who report that many couples engage in bitter arguments as a back-handed way of seeking closeness. Since marriage is a context where affect is expected to be shared, messages will be sent for this purpose even though the affect may be negative. Note especially that messages resulting in negative affect generally occur in the absence of what is positive. If couples are not sending and receiving messages of nurturance and support, then any criticism, sarcasm, withdrawal, blaming, anger, ridicule, belittling, or indifference tends to be identified as a message intended to arouse similarly negative feelings. The consequences are invariably harmful; the most that can be said for these tactics is that they do indeed produce shared feelings (however miserable) and thus they successfully achieve their purpose.

At this point it may be apparent that couples can make a choice. Knowing, for example, that most of us seek positive affect, a receiver can make the effort to recognize messages with this intent and respond in kind. Couples who do this share love and warmth. They understand that negative-sounding messages may, in a paradoxical way, be seeking positive feelings. They also understand that even if the sender is seeking *negative* affect, it is more constructive to give a positive response. There is only one situation where this is inappropriate. Sometimes a positive response to a negative message will not change the original sender's intentions to more positive ones, but instead will actually increase the criticism, blaming, or other negative messages. Obviously, when positive responses only serve to increase or maintain undesirable behavior, some other approach must be tried.

What we do to seek shared feelings is largely defined by our society and our family, because these influences shape the possible ways we act toward each other. As was suggested at the beginning of this discussion, an individual's background and previous learning may lead him or her to use uniquely personal methods of asking for shared affect. Exploring such differences is in itself a way for marriage partners to express their mutual attention and interest. It can also help them strengthen their marriage by learning to "read" the diverse but unique code each uses to seek love and support.

Power

Marital power is the capacity to exert an influence on the total relationship, including the way two people act toward each other, the activities they engage in together, and the timing and responsibility for getting joint tasks done. Sometimes two people select certain tasks and place one in charge. Sometimes they share power and work out appropriate means to give each a portion of responsibility. And sometimes they create a relationship where neither has power and little, except what is absolutely necessary, gets accomplished.

People use power in several different ways. Some individuals actively wish to possess it and to exert influence on other people. Some simply do not wish to be controlled by others, and thus exhibit powerful behavior as means of avoiding the necessity to submit to anyone else's influence. Still others do not care very much for overt coercive types of power, wishing instead to exert influence through more subtle means. Whatever his or her style may be, everyone has a personalized strategy that comes into play when marriage begins.

To correctly interpret messages that are intended to result in power, it is important to recognize the strategy used by the individual. Those who wish to have power over others, for example, send different messages than those who wish to avoid being controlled. People who wish to possess power will typically send messages of reward or punishment to control how others use their time. Such individuals also seem to think that only one person at a time can have power. They conclude—though their logic is of dubious merit—that if one marriage partner has it, the other cannot. These individuals then send power messages designed to tell their partners what to do and how to do it. For example, some messages may focus on how a spouse should dress, walk, or talk. Others may focus on the way the sender is treated, as by telling the other to pay more attention, be more responsive, be more patient, and so forth. Generally, messages from people seeking power are concerned exclusively with how other people act. These are "you" messages, seldom referring to the sender's own feelings or behavior.

Those who wish to avoid being controlled by other people also communicate in a characteristic style. Most of their messages are designed to disallow another's influence, and their strategy for achieving this questionable purpose is to undermine a spouse's power, usually by downgrading his or her ability to perform tasks, make decisions, or be a good mate. Thus they attempt to demonstrate the overall incompetence of the other person by nagging, detracting, ridiculing, or belittling. It should be remembered that the intent in this case is not to *obtain* power; instead, the person's purpose is to avoid letting someone else have it. As a result, however, the sender again largely ignores his or her own behavior, although it may actually be as incompetent as the receiver's is said to be, or more so.

There are people who do not actually wish to possess power over others. Instead, they develop a form of internal power that comes from being consistent with their own preferences. This type of person typically sends messages designed to enable him or her to stay within self-imposed limits of behavior. These messages will be fairly clear statements of who is sending what message to whom. Many, for example, will include the words "I" or "my" and will be phrased in terms of wants, preferences, or opinions. When a speaker says, "In my opinion . . . ," or "I think . . ." he or she is sending a message about wishing to be internally consistent. These verbal statements are generally accompanied by a self-disclosed emotion, more clearly revealing the feelings the sender associates with the verbal message—for example, "I think we should buy a new car rather than remodel the home because I am tired of repairing the one we have." In these messages, power of one or both partners is implied, if it is not overtly evident. The person is concerned with expressing his or her thoughts and desires, rather than with trying to impose them on others. A receiver can identify this kind of power message by listening to a sender's words and watching the sender's actions. If these are consistent, the receiver can recognize that the sender is willing to share power and influence, and need only respond by reflecting a similar attitude.

Meaning

"Meaning," as used by Kantor and Lehr, does not refer to the meaning of words, such as one obtains from a dictionary. Instead, it refers to an understanding of relationships between ideas or events, particularly those that relate to the value of one's life, one's contribution to others, or one's productivity in work or career. In this sense, communicating to obtain meaning may be the same as acquiring insight or awareness, but almost always it will also be associated with the intention of reaffirming one's worth. When we seek meaning from another, we obtain fulfillment only when both understanding and a sense of worth result.

There are at least three general types of meaning that couples seek from marriage. *Intrapersonal* meanings are those related to ideas, beliefs, and values held by the individual. This collection of meanings is commonly called one's identity. Each marital partner seeks to reaffirm the ideas and beliefs that are already part of his or her identity, and to incorporate new ones into it. Because of the intensely interwoven nature of marriage relationships, the couple also seek to learn *interpersonal* meanings, or insights about their union. Thus each seeks to find and transmit meaning about "us." Frequently, an observer may hear a husband or wife say, "we think . . ." or "we believe . . .," even though only one person is speaking; the comment refers to a shared or marital meaning. When both agree and believe similar things about their union, either can speak for both with confidence. When they disagree about marital meanings, however, both tend to be fearful, and neither partner will let the other make a "we" statement without additional comment, rebuttal, or argument.

The third type of meaning husbands and wives seek in marriage pertains to the external world. This includes beliefs about other people, whether these be relatives, neighbors, or collective groups such as politicians, clergy, or lawyers. These beliefs are called one's *world view*, and in marriage there is typically a strong impulse to seek meaning from each other about the view each possesses of the world outside their marriage.

Intrapersonal Meaning.   Rarely in life does a situation hold greater promise of determining one's worth than marriage does. The close nature of the marriage relationship brings forward the most profound elements of identity, and exposes them either to confirmation or to the struggle and despair of neglect and rejection. Marriage thus affords the possibility of greater and more intense learning about oneself than other relationships or situations. This may explain why even today, despite the prevalence of divorce, marriage is still seen as a viable lifestyle, and increasing numbers of people marry and remarry. It seems that most of us will continue to search for the circumstances that tell us about ourselves with sufficient intensity for us to be able to believe our experience. And marriage provides those circumstances.

A particularly important area in which meaning is sought is that of sex-role identity. The growing and maturing of male and female results in the acquisition of many ideas about maleness and femaleness. While some of these beliefs may be unique to an individual, it is also true that a culture labels and defines certain characteristics as inherent in being a man or woman.

Many messages sent by a husband or wife are designed to confirm that each is acting appropriately within a sex role. A man, for example, may want his wife to be sexually responsive, may loudly assert his opinion, may emphasize his ability to provide for his family and avoid doing "women's work," all as ways of seeking confirmation of his masculinity. In like manner, a woman encountering a man may utilize his maleness to obtain validation of her identity as a female. Since in marriage it is not possible to avoid communicating about the sex-role identity of each person, couples can enhance marital communication by recognizing this aspect of the need for meaning. A frequent way of seeking meaning about sex roles is to attribute certain characteristics to one or the other sex—"Men are just like that," or "Women always cry," for example. The danger in this is that we may categorize and label too quickly, and superimpose on the individual partner an unfair stereotype. Instead of trying to place an action of a wife or husband in a female or male category, it is far better to communicate with a purpose of learning what is feminine about this particular woman or masculine about this man.

Beyond the sex-role identity, both people enter marriage believing they have certain personality traits—that they are kind, hard-working, decisive, strong, loving, sloppy, or easy-going, for example. These aspects of one's identity are often subjected to scrutiny in hopes that meaning can be obtained. In marriage, the meanings obtained result from comparing one's self-perception with the other's view. For instance, a husband will send messages to his wife for the purpose of comparing his self-identity with her view of him. This occurs in both positive and negative ways, as the following example illustrates.

> Tom Reynolds was reared in a family where little affection was displayed, where frequent criticism and harsh discipline was the rule. He grew up believing he was neither loved nor lovable, even though he desired to be so. When he married, his expectations included being cared for, even doted on, by his wife. Since he believed he was not lovable, however, he found it hard to trust the authenticity of loving messages sent by his wife. Accordingly, he gradually developed little strategies to test her affection. These included claiming that she didn't love him, making plans and seeing if she complied

with exactness, and demanding that she give undivided and frequent personal and passionate sexual attention.

These strategies were used by Tom to obtain some meaning about whether or not he was loved and lovable. Unfortunately, instead of getting what he wanted, he created a paradoxical condition in which, if his wife responded as planned, her actions were discounted because they had been set up by him. If, on the other hand, she inadvertently or consciously avoided complying with his plans, he interpreted her actions as nonloving, and thus confirmed his doubts about himself. While this example shows how one might try to obtain meaning about an undesirable part of an identity, it also shows that our meaning-seeking messages may have some built-in validation of whatever we already believe about ourselves.

If a couple wish to correctly interpret messages seeking meaning, they need to become more aware of each other's self-identity. After all, most of a person's actions are, in a sense, attempts to represent an identity to another. Thus, to understand a sender's messages a receiver needs to consider, "How does this person view or think of himself or herself?" It then becomes easier to answer the question, "What does she mean?" or "What is he really saying?"

Marital Meaning. When a union of two people is formed, both bring to it their separate ideas about what the relationship will be like. As it continues and evolves, both acquire additional beliefs about the two of them as a unit. The meaning people eventually derive from marriage exists on at least two levels. The first level consists of more specific beliefs or ideas—for example, "We love each other," "We can solve problems," or "We really work well together." The second level consists of beliefs about the first level of beliefs. Couples may find that they agree or disagree on various statements that might be made about their marriage, and if they differ in what they think, they may find the differences acceptable or unacceptable. Some husbands and wives believe that differences reflect distance and unhappiness. Others can tolerate discrepancies and do not view differences as signs of disloyalty. On both levels, the specific and the higher level, couples communicate to find meaning. Essentially, each asks, "What is our marriage like to you?" Then, after obtaining several varied answers to that question, each also asks, "Do we view our marriage in the same way or differently?" Both types of information are sought after through the interaction between the two.

One way of gaining information and meaning about the marriage is through the impression each partner forms when they are together. If a wife, for instance, seems happy and content in the presence of her husband, he usually concludes she considers the marriage a happy one. Another source of meaning is the amount of talking. If a couple frequently talk and spend time alone, some meanings are obtained that are different from those obtained when a couple talk infrequently. As a result of talking often and pleasantly they will probably conclude they have a lot in common, can "talk about anything," and/or can successfully solve problems.

One sort of message seems to be used more frequently than any other to obtain marital meaning. This message is a direct request by one partner for an evaluation of how he or she performs the role of wife or husband. It appears in several ways: "Do I please you?" "Do you think we are happy?" "Do we have as good a marriage as our neighbors?" All of these and many others reflect the desire to obtain some meaning about the marital union.

When people conjointly experience things as do a husband and wife, it seems important for them to discuss that shared experience. It seems important to learn whether one's own emotional reactions are understandable or comparable to those of the other person. It seems important to express how each may experience their association, and to learn the other's feelings about being in this marriage. This kind of communication helps to make marriage meaningful.

World Views.   Included in the development of social beings is the formation of many ideas about our society or the world around us. By the time we marry, each of us has a well-organized body of these ideas to bring into the relationship. As time passes, and each partner associates not only with the other but also with the "world" of friends, neighbors, government, and work, a desire emerges to share experiences and compare notes. Couples communicate in part because the two people seek new meaning about themselves and their world. Most of the time this kind of message is easily recognized. When a partner initiates discussion of career plans, politics, religious activities, school activities, or children, the purpose in doing so is usually to learn about or share something in the social environment.

Though quite easily recognized, these messages should not be thought unimportant. Our natural curiosity and interest in things around us impel us to seek knowledge about the environment in which we live. When marriage affords opportunities for each person to obtain these meanings we usually find it fulfilling. Happy is the couple who bring to each other creative and thoughtful ideas about the world around them.

INTERACTION STYLES
AND INTERPRETING MESSAGES

To this point it has been suggested that interpreting marital messages depends in large part on whether the receiver knows the sender's purpose. Beyond being able to identify why a person is communicating, however, there is another aspect of marriage that affects whether we clearly hear and respond. Because there are two people involved, one person's actions (including speech) are followed in close sequence by the other's. This may be called an exchange. As a result of many such exchanges, each partner gradually forms images or views of the other person. Subsequently, the image or view each has of the other affects how messages are interpreted.

There probably is something to the notion that exchanges in each marriage are unique. But there are some similar characteristics in every relationship, and these can be used to help us understand more about our own communication. One particularly fruitful way of looking at the nature of exchanges is provided by Gregory Bateson (1942). As an anthropologist he was observing some tribes native to New Guinea. He noticed they interacted or exchanged behavior in different ways. For example, when members of tribe A shook their spears and yelled at members of tribe B, the people of tribe B gradually became more submissive and less belligerent. Surprisingly, the more submissive tribe B acted, the angrier tribe A became, and so on in cyclical fashion. Eventually, a fight broke out. Bateson also noted that individual members within these tribes acted in other opposite ways. When one was quiet and in the spectator role, the other was expressive. When one was tidy and clean the other tended to be sloppy and careless. From his observations he concludes that one style or type of communicational exchange between people is *complementary*, because it occurs in "opposites." While the dimensions of the opposites may vary from marriage to marriage, some complementary exchanges tend to occur in every relationship. A few common opposites are:

dominant-submissive
talkative-quiet
depressed-hopeful
sloppy-clean

Many other such opposites can exist in marriage, but these will serve as examples of the basic idea.

Bateson also noticed other interactional exchanges. When members of tribe A shook their spears and yelled at members of tribe C, the tribe C members yelled right back in an identical way. Whatever people from tribe A did, those from tribe C immediately followed suit. Such antics soon led to an escalated aggression and a fight occurred between them. Because the actions of both tribes appeared to be identical, Bateson refers to this type of communication as *symmetrical*. Other authors (Watzlawick, Beavin, and Jackson, 1967; Lederer and Jackson, 1968) have observed that symmetrical interaction is marked by competitiveness and fear of losing. Both try to be right and push responsibility on the other. To some extent, every marriage contains symmetrical behavior and this, like complementary interaction, influences how each person perceives the other.

A third type or style of interaction that Bateson observed has not, until recently, been explained as well as the others. In this, which he calls a *parallel* form of interaction, two people exhibit greater variation in their actions. At the time when a husband is discouraged, for example, a wife may be calm (not opposite), and similarly, when she is distressed, he may be comforting. Parallel behavior is neither opposite nor identical; that is, rather than interlocking with or mirroring the partner's behavior, it takes shape alongside the partner's behavior in somewhat independent fashion. Thus there is no set pattern of "oppositeness" or "identicalness." People in parallel interaction are generally flexible and cooperative. On the other hand, as we shall see in Chapter 9, they may encounter certain problems in relating to each other at an intimate level. As with complementary and symmetrical behavior, every marriage contains some parallel behavior.

One person alone does not create the style of interaction, for, by definition, an exchange includes actions of each in juxtaposition. Quite frequently this point goes either unrecognized or disregarded. Many people prefer to neglect their own actions and focus only on the other person. Wives who try to maneuver husbands, husbands who attend to what wives do or do not do are failing to see the whole picture if they do not see that the acts of each partner are responded to by the other in an opposite, identical, or different way. Both people contribute to defining what a relationship is like and both influence how they act toward each other.

Since both people share in determining the nature of the exchanges between them, receivers of messages need to add a further dimension to their interpretation. In the very act of listening to single statements and looking for the purpose or intention as suggested in the previous sections, they are exchanging behavior in a complementary, symmetrical, or parallel manner. Typically, people are more aware of *what* a person is trying to communicate than they are of the style in which messages are exchanged. But the predominant style employed within a marriage will largely shape how a husband or wife perceive each other. Some examples of this are shown in Table 1.

Table 1
INTERACTION STYLES AND PERCEPTIONS OF MARITAL PARTNERS

Predominant Interaction Style	Typical Perception of Marital Partners
Complementary	a) One person views the other as passive, unresponding, indifferent, less knowledgeable, in need of nurturance, and difficult to make decisions with. b) One person views the other as controlling, insensitive, exploitive, critical, difficult to talk to, hard to make agreements with.
Symmetrical	Both view each other as competitive, argumentative, unwilling to listen. To each the other is generally to blame, the other should change to make things better, the other is uncaring and harsh. Neither will talk about himself or herself, so each views the other as unwilling to share, desiring instead to be fairly distant. Each tends to view the other as trying to obstruct things.
Parallel	Each person tends to be perceived according to his/her unique personal attributes. Perceptions will vary consistent with different situations but both tend to be viewed as having weaknesses which are acceptable, as being caring and concerned, as being cooperative.

It should be emphasized again that all three types of interaction are present to some degree in every marriage. But in situations where symmetrical interaction exists, people's perceptions of each other will be different from those that emerge in situations where interaction is complementary or parallel. If couples wish to achieve good communication they can identify when they interact in each of the three styles and determine how their views of each other are influenced by each kind of experience.

The cyclical nature of marital communication is illustrated in Figure 1. Both people communicate for a purpose and do so in a style which influences how each perceives the other. In the light of the exchange, each evaluates whether the purpose has been achieved, and this leads to another round of each communicating for a purpose.

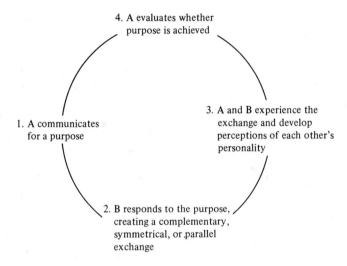

Figure 1
The circular process of marital communication.

It is important to note this cycle exists for good as well as poor communication. Good communication is likely to result when couples correctly interpret each other's intentions and exchange messages in a parallel fashion. Poor communication, in contrast, is likely to develop when either or both fail to correctly interpret the purposes of a sender's messages and, as a result, exchange behavior in a complementary (opposite) or symmetrical (identical) way. In either good or poor communication, the exchanges shape the perceptions each has of the other, and these in turn influence the further stages in the communication episode. But whereas good communicators tend to get their desired objectives, poor communicators do not. Unfortunately, failure does not usually lead poor communicators to change their methods.

It should be apparent that improvement of communication can occur by beginning at any stage of the cycle. If a couple more accurately interpret each other's messages, they probably will adjust the way they exchange behavior and alter their perceptions of each other accordingly. Or if they modify the style of their exchanges toward an increase in parallel behavior, then the view each has of the other will likewise change and messages may be more accurately received. Finally, it seems that a change in the way one (or both) views the other will lead to a modification of how messages are interpreted, with subsequent effects on the style of their exchanges. In other chapters of this book, we suggest some ways of creating better marital communication, using these three approaches.

CHAPTER
3
THE LANGUAGE OF INTIMACY AND UNDERSTANDING

Usually when we speak, we want the listener to believe and act upon what we say. Our communication is intended to *influence*. In marriage, however, using words to exert influence represents only one purpose. When one partner feels strong emotions that are closely tied to the other's feelings, there is a compelling urge to make the other understand those emotions. Achieving *understanding* is the purpose behind this form of communication.

Being understood is something that most of us hope to find in marriage. We live within the boundaries of our own lives so much of the time, and we sense that we get beyond these boundaries when a loved one knows our feelings and ideas. Somehow, being understood reassures us that our individual experience is not too strange nor different, since it is within the realm of another's comprehension.

In the rapid pace of marital life, however, we sometimes forget that understanding each other is a worthy goal. Then, when one partner wishes to share something, the other reacts as if a problem needs solving or major steps need to be taken to correct something. Instead, the listener needs only to give focused attention, and learn about the internal experience of the person talking.

Why try to understand? We are thrown together in so many ways, involving things and people other than ourselves, that if we fail to pay attention to what happens within us we imply that it is less important. But usually, after jointly attending to other things, a man and woman will recognize the neglect of themselves and seek to communicate their feeling that the two who make the marriage are as important as work, housekeeping, child care, and career. Understanding is the sharing and joining of two people, the foundation for genuine intimacy. If one of the partners feels misunderstood, little sense of intimacy will be felt.

The following is an example of the failure to understand:

Because the Caponns had been married for twenty-five years, all their friends thought the marriage was a good, if not very happy, relationship. They did many things together: traveling, working around the house, participating in sports. Almost everyone was surprised when Tom announced he was getting a divorce. Helen sought counseling help and Tom agreed to participate. Through questioning and observation, the counselor learned that Helen almost always talked more than Tom and even spoke for him, telling the counselor what Tom thought and felt. When the counselor mentioned this, Helen said she had tried to get Tom to talk more but he "just wouldn't." It was apparent that neither understood much about the other. For example, they had one child, but Helen reported that while she had always wanted more—and could have had them—Tom had wanted her to work. She explained how sad she had been because they had not had more children. When asked his opinion, Tom reported being unaware that his wife had wanted more children. He had been under the impression that she thought her career more important. When both thought they understood, it was apparent that neither did. Having felt unfulfilled, Tom wanted to end the marriage. Eventually they divorced.

One could reasonably ask, "How could they live together for twenty-five years and not understand each other?" The answer is, they probably did understand a good many things by reason of their association; however, they had never convinced themselves that they were understood, and being understood without knowing it does not help much. Not knowing we are understood occurs more commonly than one might think. Symptoms are the tendency of both people to avoid discussing matters that in the past have caused trouble, the tendency of each to accuse the other of an inability to understand, the belief of one that he or she is "dying inside," and the practice of allowing "busy work" to interfere with spending quality time together.

On the other hand, when we believe we are understood we are more likely to seek intimate experiences as a means of creating an emotional bond. In popular usage "intimacy" refers chiefly to the sexual experience, but as it is used here, the term might best be defined as *a marital experience during which both know simultaneously that they are sharing a personal and private event that strikes a responsive chord in the other.* An individual may well feel something deeply and profoundly, but intimacy involves experiencing that same feeling in the presence of a loved one who acknowledges a similar experience. It binds two people together in a way that enriches and fulfills both. In general, a husband and wife who have shared the deep satisfaction of an intimate experience will cooperatively seek to reproduce the experience. Thus intimacy is a sign of effective communication in happy marriage.

TAKING ADVANTAGE OF OPPORTUNITIES TO TALK

Almost from birth we watch how others react to us, and on the basis of our observations we form beliefs about ourselves. If, for example, we see others smile and respond pleasantly and positively, we generally think we are pleasant and worthwhile. There are some relationships in which this phenomenon is most pronounced. In marriage, for example, each partner makes an implicit agreement to be the other's primary source of affirmation by understanding and sharing intimacy. It is almost as if we agree to "act in a way that confirms the self-view of the other."

Understanding and intimacy will not develop if two people do not spend time with each other. Furthermore, the time spent must include positive involvement, where both are listened to and both contribute. This activity is an important one in and of itself. There need not be a purpose or objective other than being together, enjoying it, and finding fulfillment in each other. Consider how often in a week a couple discuss money, children, career, friends, or other topics. Opportunities to talk may be limited in some marriages, but if the time together does not include attention to personal experiences of each, then the quality of the marriage is likely to suffer.

Since understanding depends on spending time interacting with each other, a multitude of ways exist by which one person may avoid intimacy and in so doing deny his or her partner the confirmation of a desired self-concept. One of the most potent and most often used methods is to withdraw from interaction. The withdrawal can be physical, or it can be verbal and/or emotional. Common withdrawal strategies include taking all of the blame for something, distracting the communication into an irrelevant area, failing to talk at all, and dishonestly pretending to feel something not actually felt. Many withdrawal attempts are so subtle as to be nearly imperceptible. But they still have an effect. To a greater or lesser degree, the one who has risked extending or sharing, and who is therefore involved more than the other, is denied confirmation.

When either partner can see that the costs of involvement are high, this tendency to distance oneself may appear. But withdrawal, far from communicating little or no meaning, is most often perceived as rejection, revenge, or indifference. Therefore, when either or both partners see that distancing has occurred, unfortunate things begin to happen. To get involvement, some couples may even provoke fights by searching for a sore point and irritating it until a reaction is achieved. The partners neglect to emphasize the positive, and each lives virtually insulated from the other.

Much of this could be prevented if a couple establish an agreement disallowing withdrawal or distance. Such an agreement should not permit one or the other to brutalize and hurt, but should require both to stay in the conversation. When both agree to remain, the probability for achieving understanding is increased.

SELF-DISCLOSURE AND INTIMACY

As children, many of us were taught to control rather than express our feelings. And some of us were trained so effectively that, as adults, we cannot fully express feelings about things, and may not even be conscious that an emotion exists. But self-disclosure—translating our emotional experience into words and actions so it is available to someone else—is a prerequisite for understanding in marriage. And rather than being the task of one person, true self-disclosure is an activity for two or more. In the words of Colbert (1968), it is a process requiring "two to see one." This mutual sharing of personal experience is a means of achieving understanding because over time both partners have access to two kinds of important information about each other: what the other says and what can be observed. If one partner does not self-disclose, the spouse is left to make guesses about the meaning of actions. And because interpretations based solely on observation are not always reliable, accurate understanding may be more difficult to achieve.

To adequately self-disclose, each person must learn to talk about things being experienced—and about the reasons behind wanting to talk about those things. Thus, attempts to self-disclose should come when there is time to explore the ground fully and completely.

Accurate self-disclosure allows another to comprehend—and to acknowledge—what life is like. Mutual self-disclosure can accomplish several things. First, sharing an optimal amount of information will produce useful and relevant things to talk about. Second, each individual's perception of the other will be improved because it is now based on words as well as actions. Third, disclosing how one feels is an implicit statement of trust in the other person's ability to handle what is heard. An impressive number of people think they are doing their marital partner a favor by hiding worry or other intense feelings. But, because each partner subjects the other to a constant intense scrutiny, few such attempts at concealment escape attention. Since the truth is being withheld, the uninformed partner—who cannot exist without believing *something* about the other—may well misinterpret the signs. Then, in the inevitable confrontation, the "real feelings" come out. Active self-disclosing can prevent confrontation designed to get at the "real feelings." Accurate and optimal self-disclosure will reduce conflict, increase confidence, and facilitate understanding.

ACKNOWLEDGING RECEPTION OF THE TOTAL MESSAGE

Messages between husband and wife contain at least two levels: the literal meaning of the words, and the manner in which they are said. Bateson (1935) describes these two characteristics as the "report" and the "command." The words people say *report* what is meant, and the tone of the voice, facial expressions, gestures, and so forth *command* or tell the listener how to interpret the words. Listening effectively and understanding requires that both the report and the command be received and acknowledged.

Customarily—probably because it seems easier—we listen to and acknowledge only one level of the message. In effect, we say either "I understood your words," or "I heard the command." An example can help illustrate. Suppose Harold and Mary are having difficulty sexually and both know it, and in an angry tone of voice, Harold says, "You are not responsive to me." Mary will probably acknowledge only the command in Harold's message, and snap back, "You are never gentle and considerate of me." This is a response to his anger and not to his words. At another time the same couple may be talking about their social life when Mary excitedly says, "I really like to dance and be alone with you." Harold may ignore or fail to perceive Mary's command and reply only to her words by saying, "Dancing is all right I guess, but I like to talk with other people." In both cases, understanding is not achieved because the receiver does not acknowledge hearing both the meaning of the words and the command. Had this occurred, Mary might have said, "I can hear you want me to be more responsive, and I would like to be, but when you are angry about the way I am, I don't feel close to you." Or Harold might have said, "I can see you really like to dance."

Besides acknowledging two levels in a specific message, understanding depends on listening to and acknowledging changes of focus in the conversation. For instance, at parties, discussion meetings, and dinners, people talk about rather conventional topics: politics, business, religion, current events. And in such circumstances, responding in a logical and topical way is not only permissible but in accordance with the expectations of others. In marriage, however, each time the husband and wife talk they also send messages about themselves and things that occur between them. Thus, because both are involved in the same relationship at an intense emotional level, the focus of conversation may at any time shift from the current topic to some aspect of their relationship. Whenever statements about money management, sex, and child-rearing are made, good listeners tune in to what is meant about their relationship as well as to what is said about the topic.

Conversation between a couple may be likened to a chain whose links consist of statements made by each in turn. When they talk about a conventional topic, each partner initially focuses on the topic and what he or she has previously said. The links are only loosely joined. But as soon as a comment by one person suggests a chain of thought that is important to the two of them, each person's responses become more firmly linked to the other's. The example at the top of the next page shows how this occurs. (The solid lines show the statements most attended to.)

Notice in the example that as long as the conversation focuses on the topic, each speaker gives more attention to his or her own train of ideas than to the other person's. That is, comments 1, 3, and 5 would be more logically ordered if they stood alone than they are when intertwined with the listener's 2, 4, and 6. But after comment 6, sender and listener start to respond more directly to

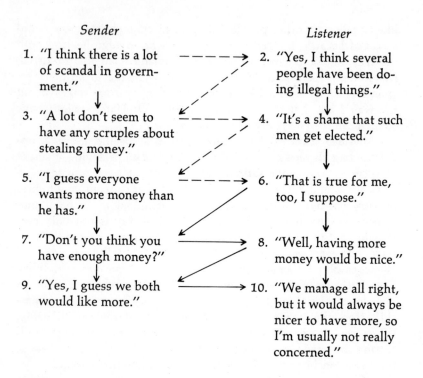

Sender   *Listener*

1. "I think there is a lot of scandal in government."

2. "Yes, I think several people have been doing illegal things."

3. "A lot don't seem to have any scruples about stealing money."

4. "It's a shame that such men get elected."

5. "I guess everyone wants more money than he has."

6. "That is true for me, too, I suppose."

7. "Don't you think you have enough money?"

8. "Well, having more money would be nice."

9. "Yes, I guess we both would like more."

10. "We manage all right, but it would always be nicer to have more, so I'm usually not really concerned."

each other. When one implies that he or she wants more money, the conversation changes focus, and each person gives increased attention to what the other person has said or implied.

In communication whose purpose is to promote understanding, there are various responses that help to show that one has received the total message—which means, on the one hand, acknowledging reception of both the report and the command and, on the other hand, recognizing when a shift in focus is intended. These responses are as follows.

★ *Reflective Listening.* A message that seeks to label the feeling of the person speaking. "You seem quite happy about that." Reflections almost always contain an emotion word.

★ *Clarifying.* A statement that combines the meaning and the intention of the message. "I'm understanding you to say that you think I manage money all right, but that you get concerned about it."

★ *Inquiring.*   A statement that collects more information about the meaning or the intent of a message. "I would like you to tell me more about that."

★ *Observing.*   A statement describing some nonverbal behavior of the speaker. "I notice that your voice rises when you talk about money."

★ *Disclosing.*   A statement describing the feeling of the listener while the speaker is speaking. "When you said that, I felt afraid and a little angry."

In many contexts, listening can consist only of silently paying attention to what is said, but more than that is required in marriage. Something must also be said or done to show awareness of the report, the command, and the focus. That is, although in a nonmarital relationship it may be permissible to understand someone without communicating this fact, in marriage each partner needs to *know* that he or she is understood by the other. In fact, the essence of marital listening is the acknowledgment that understanding has occurred.

PRECEDING INFLUENCE BY UNDERSTANDING

The emphasis in this chapter has been on communication for understanding. Let us now relate this to those types of communication that are intended to influence other people.

Much marital communication is designed to bring about change in a partner's behavior, whether by coercion, blaming, accusations, educating, asking, or bribery. The communication problem that arises is that usually, when we see overt attempts to change us, we cease listening very well, and then, after failing to understand, we become defensive. This leads to one of the great ironies of human behavior, for a defensive, anxious person tends to be unreceptive to information and may respond instead with attempts to change the first person! The cycle that emerges is: (1) low information, (2) poor understanding, (3) anxiety, and (4) attempts to change the other person, who in turn is caught up in the cycle also. Thus the cycle of misunderstanding and low information tends to engulf both partners and perpetuate itself. There is a way to interrupt such cycles, however, and that is to follow the principle of collecting information before attempting to exert influence or control.

Suppose, for example, that a couple have learned to collect information before reacting to criticism that is made carelessly and perhaps too strongly. When the sender perceives that the hearer is trying to understand, rather than sending back a message in kind, several positive results occur. First, anxiety is typically reduced because no conflict is apparent. Second, the hearer is perceived as being more receptive to what is being said. Third, it is possible to see the potential for working together toward a solution. In short, the effort to understand, when perceived as a cooperative gesture, can pave the way for efforts to promote change.

There are two viewpoints from which the principle of collecting information can be applied. These are from the position of a person who wants change to occur and the position of the person who is being asked to change or to participate in cooperative change.

Suppose the sender, who wishes things to improve, identifies a situation where change is desired. A correct application of the principle suggests that before telling the receiver how to change, the sender should try to learn how the same situation is viewed by the other person. Thus the sender needs to ask questions and get some idea of what the receiver thinks and feels before proceeding to explain what modifications are hoped for. By seeking to understand the other person, the sender can help preserve a feeling of closeness.

From the vantage point of the receiver, the principle also helps to preserve intimacy. When a sender makes a request for change, or otherwise tries to influence, the receiver can, instead of reacting defensively, simply ask, "What do you mean?" or "Tell me more about it." Doing so tells the sender that communication is possible. It also, paradoxically, helps the receiver *feel* less defensive. The result on both sides is a tendency to stop blaming and start working toward mutual understanding. In the long run, the goal of understanding is of paramount importance, so it is well for couples to practice trying to understand before trying to influence.

OVERCOMING BARRIERS TO INTIMACY AND UNDERSTANDING

When we marry, few of us are ready to move rapidly into total intimacy. Achieving understanding and intimacy is a gradual process, often requiring several years. In some marriages it is never really achieved.

Having been treated to the hardening experiences of our upbringing, most of us come to marriage armed with certain behaviors we can use to fend off intimacy if it becomes too risky. Unfortunately, the behaviors that serve this purpose have a generally inhibiting effect and we tend to use them even when we do not wish to put up barriers. However, despite our protestations or attempts to rationalize otherwise, it is largely our own fear or lack of skill that holds us back from more open expression of our feelings. The question we face is whether we can overcome our own inhibitions.

A high level of closeness cannot be achieved in every relationship. But it is desirable for us to extend ourselves with our partner in marriage if we wish to make this union our chief source of fulfillment. One way to begin is to make a point of telling each other about our positive feelings, for these are most easily accepted by another person and thus pose little risk. For example, when a wife feels warm because of her husband's kindness or when a husband feels cared for as a result of his wife's attention this should be shared. Obviously, inhibition is reduced and intimacy becomes easier when couples express their tender feelings rather than withholding them. Failing this, they risk being like the crusty old Scotsman who stood at his wife's graveside lamenting her death and saying, "Aye, she was a good woman and I nearly told her once."

Our inhibitions about revealing other kinds of feelings are harder to overcome. We are afraid of being criticized or ridiculed, and so we try to display only the feelings we think are acceptable—emotions which, if they are not approved of, are at least not embarrassing. The fear of self-disclosure ranges from a deep dread which blocks all expression to only minor discomfort. In most people, it can be overcome by progressive exposure—in other words, by beginning with those expressions that involve less risk, then gradually obtaining confidence to disclose more. The turning point, where fear is overcome, is reached when the person who is afraid of intimacy discloses that very fear and receives acceptance.

Fortunately, the process of achieving intimacy is a gradual one, extending into many marital years. The actions that promote intimacy provide the magic that makes marriage a renewing and vital relationship. To experience that magic, however, both husband and wife must value understanding and intimacy, not only as a means of attaining other goals, but also as an objective that is worthy in itself.

CHAPTER
4
SEXUAL
COMMUNICATION

As a couple develop, enlarge, and refine their marriage, their sexual experience also needs to evolve and change. At the beginning sex may be exciting and erotically fulfilling, but repeated experience tends to produce a feeling of sameness. What is needed is to expand the range of sexual expression, bringing more of each person's total personality into play. Unless this happens, sex will be less than it can be and a couple will be mutually less satisfied. The task for most of us, then, is to find a way to improve our sexual lives as our marriage grows in other areas. To do this we first need to improve the way we communicate about sex.

More than anything else, sexual behavior is itself a form of communication, one of the most profound sources of meaning because it is related to more facets of the human personality than any other. Some marriages seem to be relatively successful without accurate sexual communication; by and large, however, the quality of the sexual relationship affects and is affected by almost every other aspect of a couple's relationship. For this reason, sexual expression needs to consist of clear messages that effectively communicate the feelings of both partners. Sexual pleasure that is freely given, in an honest and mutually intimate way, can draw two people together into a loving and passionate bond that is continually strengthened, enhancing the marriage.

There are some distinct advantages derived from viewing sex as communication. We become more aware of its complexities and intricacies, as opposed to focusing on physical or mechanical procedures. This allows us to conclude we will never utilize all its potential, and leads us to more fully explore its possibilities, so that it need not be repetitious or boring. Thinking of the sexual relationship as communication also permits us to view it as the continuous process which it is, instead of as a series of isolated events. Rather than being limited to foreplay and intercourse, it is as expansive as we care to make it.

Sexual experiences are obviously a prominent part of the marriage dialogue. Although they are not necessarily more important than other kinds of husband-wife interaction, they have a more powerful effect on us than any other. This power has a combined psychological, emotional, and physical foundation. Our sexuality is expressed in each of these domains, and all of them must be considered if a couple want to obtain the most satisfactory experience. In fact, anyone who thinks that sexual arousal is merely a physical response to physical stimuli has much to learn. We experience arousal psychologically, through pleasure centers in the brain, where sensual fantasies are brought into being. Normally, we also experience an emotional arousal, which accompanies the tactile or physical sensations. Effective sexual communication utilizes all of these and integrates them into full, rich experience.

A good sexual relationship depends first of all on mutual understanding of what is satisfying to each partner. Acquiring the necessary knowledge takes patience and cooperation because of possible differences in male and female attitudes (resulting from cultural training), because of the changing preferences of each person over time, and because of variations occasioned by mood and setting. Successful couples, though, generally reach some form of understanding—it may be unspoken—about what is pleasurable to each, how frequently intercourse will occur, what may be said about it between them and other people, who starts it, and what constitutes the "best" experience. When agreement is reached on these aspects of the relationship, both partners can feel fulfilled.

Since physical sexual responses are easy to recognize, they are often used as a gauge of success in intercourse. Techniques that have produced the desired responses for a given couple are repeated on later occasions, evolving into a style or pattern that seems to be a reliable formula for that couple. But then, after repeatedly having sex with the same partner over a period of years, it is not uncommon for either or both partners to begin feeling that something is lacking, that the formula no longer works. To find renewed fulfillment, they begin again to experiment. Having begun with the physical experience in the first place, it seems logical to again try to find fulfillment or agreement on this basis. This approach leads couples to seek more satisfaction by improving and/or varying their techniques. This is fine as far as it goes, but although new techniques may be exciting at first, a couple should attend to the emotional and psychological side of sex as well as the physical. If they can improve in all three areas they are more likely to experience renewed emotional sensitivity and psychological arousal, and thus to rekindle the passion that brings a sense of more complete sexual fulfillment.

The art of love in marriage is the art of learning to communicate sexually. Unfortunately, an exaggerated concern with the physical aspects of sex can impair our ability to communicate loving feelings and ideas related to it. If the purpose of sex is only to achieve a physical response, the physical cues given and responded to are channeled into our conscious processing system, but others more subtle are channeled out of awareness. It is possible in this way for two people to desensitize themselves to the tender and gentle nuances that can be shared when they communicate the emotional and psychological along with the physical. Sexual interaction does, after all, serve a variety of purposes. For example, it can bring release of tension and stress, be a source of fun and enjoyment, act as a means of giving support and encouragement, and be the medium for a sharing of rich intimacy. These are all possible when we expand and deepen our communication rather than restrict it to one modality.

In this chapter, our emphasis is on the emotional and psychological aspects of sexual communication. This is because there is an abundance of published material today that deals with physical techniques, and people are generally more knowledgeable about such techniques than they are about the emotional and psychological factors.

ELEMENTS OF SEXUAL EXPRESSION

It is probably not possible, nor desirable, to give an exact description of what sexual communication ought to be, because no one should feel pushed to communicate in any specific way. It may be helpful, however, to state some principles that can be adapted to fit a variety of conditions and people. We shall discuss these under five headings which correspond to important aspects of sexual expression.

Physical Performance

Successful sexual experiences require, first of all, the physical capacity to perform. There must be a penile erection and vaginal lubrication. Each partner must be capable of arousal and periodic orgasmic experience, although both can enjoy sexual encounters without them. If partial or total physical impairment exists, there will be little satisfaction because consummation will not regularly occur.

Because sex is a natural physical function, we may assume that our bodies will automatically respond as expected. Then, if one partner has difficulty in physical performance, the other is not prepared to understand and react in a helpful way. Instead, if a male is impotent, the female partner may react as though she is at fault, undesirable, or even repulsive. Similarly, if a wife is unresponsive, a man may wrongly conclude that his technique is crude or that he is otherwise inadequate.

To begin with, both partners should have some insight into the differences in the physical responses of the male and female. The research done to date suggests that females are more responsive to tactile stimuli than to visual, and that they often require more time for arousal than do males. The first sign of arousal is an increased sensitivity in erogenous areas, including the genitals, breasts, and inner thighs. This is followed by swelling of the sex organs and lubrication of the vagina, which readies it for intercourse. Continual stimulation of the clitoris, if combined with relaxed, focused participation, leads to orgasm. This consists of a spasmodic contracting of the muscles which are just below the vagina. Following one or more orgasms, the aroused and enlarged genitals return to a flaccid state. Ordinarily, this requires more time for females than does the resolution period for males.

Males, as was suggested above, are usually more aroused than females are by visual stimuli such as nudity or erotic body movements. Once stimulated with a full erection, the male, under normal circumstances, can maintain arousal until his partner is also excited. After the penis is inserted, the combination of contact between the glans penis and vaginal wall and of pressure on the penile base further stimulates the male, but he can to some extent control the escalation of excitement up to the point of emission, which consists of a contracting of the vas deferens, prostate, and seminal vesicles which ready the sperm for ejaculation. Once the emission stage is reached the male cannot voluntarily control the ejaculatory response, which is a spasmodic contracting of large muscles at the base of the penile shaft. Following ejaculation, the penis returns to a flaccid state and other signs of excitement gradually subside.

The preceding outline is highly generalized. Males and females do not invariably respond at the same rate or with the same intensity, and there is a great range in what constitutes "normal" sexual responses. Illness, fatigue, or psychological factors can affect responsiveness and prevent consummation. However, if one or both partners rarely or never reach orgasm, it is wise to investigate the physical as well as other potential causes of the difficulty. Without the capacity to function at the physical level, the couple are missing the minimal foundation for a good sexual relationship.

Communicating a Sexual Identity

It is generally accepted that humans feel sexual impulses even at a very early age. There is, however, no societal agreement on how parents should react to evidence of sexual urges shown by their children. Some people advocate thorough education to insure proper handling of sexual feelings. Others seem to think sheltering and naivety is the best approach. Still others, even in this age of understanding, think that sexual feelings should be discouraged through the use of punishment and degradation. But regardless of the parental attitude, the child who is maturing to adulthood must come to terms with the fact that he or she is a sexual being. Sexual feelings and accompanying actions are a built-in part of the personality and they cannot be totally ignored. Nor is it very desirable to try. Indeed, some element of sexual expression is present in every interpersonal relationship, and it is the history of these interpersonal dynamics, combined with inherited tendencies, that eventually determines each person's sexual needs, desires, and manner of expression. Thus to some people, for example, touching and being touched is in itself very gratifying, while to others it holds no inherent satisfaction, and some people need music, soft lights, and intimate conversation to put them "in the mood," while others prefer a more earthy approach.

The beginning of fulfilling sexual communication is the formation of stable sexual identities for a wife and husband. A sexual identity is made up of two sets of beliefs that are derived from experience. The first set includes all the beliefs we have about how *we* prefer to act, whether in giving and experiencing sexual pleasure, in expressing our femininity or masculinity, or in communicating about our sexual selves. The second set includes our beliefs about how we prefer to be acted *toward*. These beliefs may range from whether we think sexual topics should be discussed publicly to the amount of foreplay we desire. We develop full and complete sexual identities only after we have explored both kinds of preferences.

Some people think that men and women are very different in their sexual desires, and so tend to ascribe certain preferences to females and others (opposites) to males. An example of this is the outdated notion that women do not like sex as well as men, but perform it for other reasons. This notion is traceable to nineteenth century ideas of what women *ought* to want, and it successfully inhibited many women in past generations from enjoying intercourse. In fact, however, Masters and Johnson (1975) found that women are potentially more active sexual beings, having a greater if not unlimited capacity for arousal and stimulation. Women also seem to prefer to relate longer and more extensively, in a more emotionally intimate way, than do men. In general, however, men and women appear to have similar ideas, desires, and hopes for sexual experience.

Nevertheless, there remain innumerable individual variations in the ways we prefer to act and the ways we prefer that our partner act. In their book *The Pleasure Bond*, Masters and Johnson (1975) wrote the following about such preferences:

> Thus every individual evolves a unique set of needs that have to be met if satisfying sexual feelings are to result. In a sense, these needs, these factors, might be considered prerequisites to pleasure; our term for them is the sexual value system. At baseline, it includes all the considerations—the time, the place, the mood, the words used, the gestures made, the thousand and one little signals that a man and woman give each other without language—that the individual requires in order to respond emotionally, to let feelings come to the surface. (p. 42)

One may ask how we learn what we prefer. Generally, rather than learning *from* experience, we learn *what* we experience. This means we need to become aware of what we feel or how we react during sexual experiences. At the beginning we can monitor our feelings during different sexual encounters and while expressing different levels and kinds of sexual behavior. One obvious question concerns timing. Some persons will find, for example, that they enjoy intercourse most in the early morning, others that they prefer it late at night. But many other factors are also worth examining. How much embracing and touching is important during the day? What kind? Is a great deal of variation in techniques of intercourse important? Should intercourse be sustained for long-drawn-out periods, shorter times, or both? How important is it for a partner to be really "tuned in" to how we are feeling? If he or she isn't, what do we wish we could do about it?

Having identified our preferences, we must now communicate these to our partner. Because our preferences may differ from day to day, or change as we grow older, sexual communication offers the possibility of continued excitement and richness. Little of this is possible, however, if we fail to communicate our preferences to each other.

The task of communicating a sexual identity is made easier if we recognize that it cannot and will not be accomplished in one conversation, but must be made a basic part of the entire dialogue of marriage. Furthermore, it will require successfully utilizing several forms of communication, all of which add to the relationship. It is important, however, for a couple to recognize that each partner has a responsibility to keep the other informed. Neither partner should have to guess or assume anything.

Because sexual knowledge is more readily available today than in the past, we might think that communicating about sex is so easy that it will always happen. But talking about one's preferences to a sexual partner is difficult for many people. All kinds of questions may block the way, for example, "If I have to tell, is it because I am not loved enough for my partner to sense what I need and desire?" "If I make my desires known, will they be used against me?" "If I tell, will it take the spontaneity out of the experience?" "What if I tell and nothing happens?" Thus many couples avoid communicating about individual sexual preferences. Of course, it may be that the majority of their experiences are sufficiently fulfilling that little talking or explaining seems necessary. The fact remains that verbal communication is nearly always necessary to achieve the best sexual relationship. The most dramatic communication is, of course, the actual physical response of each to the other. If on a particular occasion a technique is arousing, it will probably be used again soon after, for it seems logical to assume that the partner prefers it. Moods change, however, and an attempt to recapture passion by the same method may not be successful a second time. Relying only on nonverbal cues may thus lead the partners to misjudge what is preferred. Or worse, they may conclude that sexual pleasure happens by chance and cannot be planfully created between them. But by talking about their preferences as well as using nonverbal cues, a couple can progressively reach greater pleasure and fulfillment.

How can couples begin this kind of talking? When an appropriate time can be found—*not* right after a negative, frustrating experience—partners might try telling each other what makes the best sexual experience for each. At the outset, it may be wise to focus on, "How I want to act . . . ," including the range of feelings, frequency of intercourse, whether or not to initiate, whether to experiment, the variety of techniques, desired amount of foreplay, the kind and amount of sexual interaction desired outside of intercourse (embracing, touching, and so forth). After these and other related topics are discussed, it is appropriate to also share "How I like to be treated." The same ideas can be covered here, but in addition couples can discuss one of greater importance: "Knowing that our preferences change from time to time, how do we tell each other what we desire at a particular time?" When this is fully answered to the satisfaction of each, it will increase the probability that more satisfactory adjustments can be made to the different and changing moods and preferences of each person.

Communicating Desire

The marriage bond is created in part because we hope our partner will find us most desirable among all others. Being desired by someone we love is a prominent expectation and is an important element in a positive sexual bond. Feeling attractive and desired by a lover is an impelling part of a full and complete relationship.

Rather than being limited to physical-sensual attractiveness, however, desiring and being desired relates to many aspects of marriage. An example of failure to successfully communicate desire can illustrate this.

> *Gary claimed he had but two complaints about Jean. One was that she was overweight. Trying to be considerate, he avoided berating or ridiculing her, choosing an incentive approach instead. Despite his offers of new clothes, money, and vacations, however, Jean failed to lose any weight, though she made several attempts, with Gary's help, to find a successful reducing program. Gary also complained that Jean was sexually unresponsive, even indifferent. Again, instead of being harsh or abusive, he frequently and logically discussed with her the importance of improving her sexual performance. Interestingly, she agreed that improvement was necessary, but for some reason her attempts seemed to fall short of achieving what both wanted.*

In this example, Gary was successfully, although inadvertently, communicating to his wife that he found her less than desirable. Subsequently, both Gary and Jean also assigned her the responsibility for a lack of sexual satisfaction. Jean was thus caught in a situation where she felt not only undesired but also guilty for not being a passionate partner.

It is the feeling of being desired that enables most of us to share our sexual feelings and risk giving more in our sexual encounters. Believing that we are attractive and wanted unlocks our spontaneity and helps us be increasingly sensitive to what each may prefer and hope for sexually. Knowing how to communicate desire for another person is therefore an essential and necessary part of a positive sexual experience.

Most of us know, at least minimally, how to communicate desire. We find our wife or husband naturally desirable during the early stages of marriage. The newness and pleasure of sex carries us along and we do not have to learn much else. But as time passes and work, children, and/or social activities occupy increasing amounts of time, we gradually limit our expressions of desire to the bedroom and the intercourse experience. Inevitably, some of the excitement of the marriage fades. Now, although it is often thought that a diminishment in sexual pleasure is a natural result of being married, this situation need not exist, and it does not for those couples who have recognized the importance of maintaining and, in fact, enlarging their abilities to communicate desire to each other.

It is helpful in this connection to review the findings of some researchers studying nonverbal behavior (Birdwhistle, 1970). They reported that there typically exists a series of sequential steps between a man and woman's first physical touch and their most passionate embrace. The first step is finger pressure, answered by a counterpressure, followed by intertwining of fingers, and so forth. These steps, with some individual variations, are familiar to most of us and are used in a variety of ways. During courtship, for example, a girl is able to tell if a boy is "fast" if he passes preliminary steps and attempts more advanced ones. A boy finds out when a girl is "easy" the same way—if he begins at step 1 and she responds at step 10, he can draw certain conclusions from her rapid escalation.

In marriage, this sequence is still important, but for other reasons. When husbands and wives become adept at and utilize all parts of the sequence, both experience the breadth and variety available in sexual communication. Some couples, after experiencing the power of the last steps, are ready to skip the less passionate intermediate steps as being no longer of interest. Some men or women, for example, may begin initiating sex at the last stages of the sequence, expecting their partners to respond at the same level of intensity. If this is done only on occasion, as a variation, it will not disrupt the creation of a positive sexual relationship; but if it occurs regularly it can have a harmful effect. Having failed to practice the early parts of the sequence, the couple soon neglect them altogether. This means that unless intercourse is immediately in the offing, there is no communication of physical desire. But a time when intercourse is not possible may be the very time when both need to know they are desired. If partners think only of the fact that they cannot reach the conclusion of the sexual sequence, they deprive themselves of the opportunity to fill this need. To maximize communication of desire, then, it is good for both to make frequent and pleasurable use of all parts of the sequence they practiced early in their relationship—touching fingers, holding hands, nuzzling, nibbling, and whatever else is included.

In sexually passionate marriages, desire is not limited to physical interaction. A wife communicates desire for her husband's companionship, laughter, wit, and sense of humor. A husband tells of enjoying the way his wife thinks, walks, laughs, or shares things with him. These and dozens of other aspects of each person may be desired in any marriage, but neither person will benefit much if such desire is not clearly communicated. Thus if our sexual lives are gradually becoming less exciting, one of the first things to consider is whether each is able to show desire for other aspects of a partner's company.

The newspaper columnists frequently advise that it is important to keep the courtship in our marriages. This is inadequate advice if all it means is being polite and courteous. The fact is, it was during courtship that we first experienced sexual passion for each other. Attributing this to the newness of "love" and sexual experience, we may forget that at the very time of these heightened sexual feelings we were also communicating that we found each other immensely desirable in other ways as well. Should we continue or regain this kind of communication, then we should expect to find our sexual lives correspondingly more passionate.

The Primary Sexual Responsibility

A very common view of marital sexual expression suggests that one partner is responsible for the fulfillment of the other. Many a woman still believes it is her duty, as a "warm, responsive wife," to be at her husband's beck and call. Many a man seems to believe he is sexually successful only if he causes his wife to have frequent and profound sexual experiences. In opposition to this view, Masters and Johnson (1975) wrote:

> Effective sexual functioning is something that transpires between two people. To be effective it must be done together. It is something that sexually functional couples do *with* each other, not to or for each other. (*The Pleasure Bond*, pp. 7–8)

Whenever anyone tries to do something *to* or *for* another person, the criterion of success is the reactions or performance of the other person. This condition will inevitably produce a sense of failure whenever desired responses are not forthcoming. For example, suppose a wife is, for legitimate reasons, too tired to be interested in and responsive to her husband's sexual attentions. If he considers himself responsible for her pleasure, he will experience a feeling of failure. Not only that, but since misery loves company, he will often see to it that his wife shares the blame by criticizing her lack of responsiveness and provoking further distance between them.

Feeling more responsible for someone else than we are willing to be for ourselves is seldom desirable, and in the case of marital sexual behavior it can be especially harmful. Our emotions are so varied that frequently a husband and wife do not share exactly the same feelings or experience them with the same intensity at exactly the same time. A common mistake is to try to change our own feelings at the request of our partner, or else to try to alter the other person's feelings. Such attempts merely create tension that interferes with effective sexual communication. Neither partner can relax and enjoy the other, and eventually sex seems to require more effort than any pleasure is worth.

The primary sexual responsibility each partner has is for his or her own fulfillment, because—good or bad, happy or sad, fulfilling or unfulfilling—one person's sexual experience is usually due more to his or her behavior than to the actions of the spouse. Sometimes it seems easier to take responsibility for someone else, or to default on our own share, but this is an illusion. Being responsible for ourselves means that we let the other know what we prefer and desire, whatever the occasion or situation. It also means that we act in ways that benefit the other person, but we do so for the purpose of bringing our own fulfillment into being. Contrary to what some may think, this is not the least bit selfish. The giver shares no less than the receiver, for sex is best when each person knows the other wants it.

The manner in which we exercise this self-responsibility is, however, a crucial factor. Criticizing, blaming, cajoling, pleading, or demanding are tactics that hinder sexual communication. The successful communication is that which helps each discover, value, and legitimize sexual desire.

For some individuals the exercise of self-responsibility is not easy to learn. A woman who has been taught the double standard of sex—pleasure for her husband, duty and receptivity for her— may need help in overcoming her fear of accepting sex as a legitimate source of pleasure. She will need opportunities to talk about her attitudes, to examine her feelings, and to formulate new expectations for herself. Then she will need the freedom and support to experiment without risking criticism or indifference. A man who has been taught that sexual prowess consists only in the artful performance of various techniques will similarly need opportunities to face and admit his need for gentleness and intimacy, and to enjoy the resulting passion. This makes prowess the ability to feel and share with his partner. Because their difficulties relate to attitudes as well as preferences, this man and this woman will require time to learn, to adjust, and to build toward a relationship from which both partners derive maximum satisfaction.

The Role of Cohesion

Cohesion is an interpersonal condition that results when people are aware of having shared an emotional experience. The people who are involved feel drawn together because of the perceived similarity between them. Thus two strangers, after witnessing a tragic car accident, may not only feel fear and sorrow, but they also may feel as if they had known each other for a long time.

Emotional and psychological cohesion play an important role in effective sexual expression. Sex seems to be best when a feeling of cohesion exists prior to intercourse. Perhaps this is because cohesion is a condition that helps both feel their relationship will continue, and the belief that a union will be perpetuated is conducive to sexual responsiveness. For some people, indeed, it is almost a prerequisite to free enjoyment. At any rate, because of the relationship between cohesion and sex, couples who learn to communicate outside the bedroom to produce cohesion between them will also see benefits sexually.

The most powerful builders of cohesion are crises successfully weathered together—the death or severe illness of a family member, for instance, or temporary loss of income. However, no one would wish to experience such misfortunes solely in order to draw closer together. There exist, in any case, less dramatic and more predictable ways of building cohesion. These should not be neglected, for good sexual communication often depends on a couple's ability to find a sense of cohesion by one means or another. The expression of deeply held convictions, the sharing of reflections and meditations, and joint participation in many kinds of activities are all important. Whatever the approach, quality time spent with each other will do much to draw a couple into a cohesive bond. As we mentioned in our discussion of intimacy (Chapter 3), it is then essential that they communicate *to each other* their sense that they are feeling the same things. This will enhance their total relationship and bring a greater sense of fulfillment, not only sexually, but in every aspect of the marriage.

INTEGRATING AND BALANCING THE ASPECTS OF SEXUAL COMMUNICATION

So far we have discussed cohesion, self-responsibility, communication of preferences, and communication of desire as separate aspects of a couple's sexual communication. In this section we shall show how these are interrelated and how, with a knowledge of that interrelationship, a couple can adjust their total interaction to achieve optimal fulfillment.

To begin with, let's summarize the separate elements of a fulfilling sexual relationship. As previously mentioned, they are: (a) the capacity to function physically without impairment in carrying intercourse to completion; (b) an acceptance of sexual responsibility, recognizing that each partner is primarily responsible for his or her own fulfillment and secondarily so for that of the partner; (c) creation and maintenance of an emotional bond in which two people feel mutual cohesion; (d) communication of a sexual identity, including the variations in preferences of each; (e) communication of desire for the total person. With these in mind, we can continue the discussion of how to integrate them and balance the effect each has on us.

Can we assume that all the elements are important? Obviously, if either person cannot function physically, the other elements will not make much difference. In turn, however, physical functioning is often dependent on the emotional bond, capacity for variation, and/or the recognition of one's own sexual responsibility. Consider sexual impotence in males. In rare cases this is caused by a permanent biological condition; temporary impotence may also be caused by illness or medication. Most often, however, impotence is caused by anxiety, by a fear of failing to perform adequately. Rather than believing sex is something done with a wife, an impotent male often thinks he is solely responsible for the success or failure of intercourse. The physical capacity of a woman to experience orgasm is likewise affected by whether she accepts or rejects responsibility for her own pleasure and by whether a stable and caring emotional bond exists between her and her partner.

From the foregoing, we can conclude that all elements of sexual communication are important. We can also assume that too much emphasis on one, to the exclusion of another, will eventually result in reduced pleasure and fulfillment. A husband and wife can help ensure having positive sexual experiences by paying attention to all five elements.

Since marriage is a changing ebb and flow, one or more of the elements will need periodic adjustment to restore appropriate balance. Couples have to face questions like the following: (a) How do we tell when the emotional bond is at a low level and needs improving? What can we do to improve it? (b) How will we know when we need to increase the variety of our sexual behavior? Do we give enough emphasis to foreplay, talking, kissing, and embracing? Do we focus only on intercourse? Are there some limits that one or both of us feel are important? (c) How do we help each other accept responsibility for sexual pleasure? How can we tell when one or both are failing to be responsible? What can we do to change? (d) Do both of us have a reasonable knowledge of our bodies and how we function? If not, how do we learn? Can we both talk about ourselves and each other?

The interdependence of these factors suggests that sexual enhancement occurs in a cyclical fashion, and we have depicted it this way in Figure 2. As the figure shows, a successful emotional bond promotes acceptance of sexual responsibility. This in turn contributes to optimal variation because it encourages free statements regarding sexual preferences. When these conditions are well satisfied then physical performance tends to be more passionate and successful and, to complete the cycle, this leads in turn to renewal of the emotional bond.

If we keep in mind these interrelationships, then in times of difficulty we can readjust our sexual interaction to yield more pleasure and fulfillment by doing things to improve each of the key

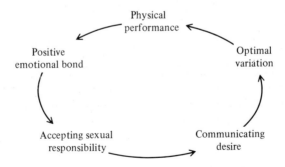

Figure 2
The cycle of sexual enhancement.

elements. Probably only one or two will need adjusting at a time. The one action to avoid is neglecting sex or withdrawing from sexual interaction altogether. Some find sex so frustrating they mistakenly try to eliminate it, but it is not possible to do so entirely in a relationship where it is legitimate and expected. Even if intercourse is discontinued, thoughts, feelings, and stimulation will still exist. Thus, when problems arise, it seems more advantageous for us to continue having intercourse—even if it falls short of ideal— while both participate in working to improve the area(s) that seem out of balance with the rest.

To improve a given area we must first recognize what is wrong and then do something to change. Table 2 (pp. 64–65) shows some common symptoms of problems and some typical solutions. These are given as examples and should be considered only a part of what may be done to improve our sexual lives.

Sexual pleasure is a worthwhile and important aspect of married life. Expressing ourselves to a loved person of the opposite sex strikes responsive feelings deep within us. Most of us can maintain a fulfilling life if we'll recognize that as one aspect of our total relationship changes, we need to make adjustments in the others. If we can together better our own ability to express and receive, we will find that the joint experience becomes better, too.

THE SEXUAL CHOICE

Traditionally, the contract of marriage limits sex to the couple. The assumption is that it is best for sex to occur in a context of a total commitment. Another view presumes that marriage is not necessarily exclusive and, if both consent, other partners may be found. Emphasis is usually given, however, to having some emotional commitment as part of any relationship that is formed. According to a yet more permissive position, sex is pleasurable and desirable in or out of marriage, in a variety of situations, with a variety of partners. In this case, sexual pleasure is the primary, perhaps only objective. These three points of view offer alternative ways to conduct our sexual lives.

Since sexual pleasure is most frequently the reason for selecting partners other than a spouse, it will also be easily recognized that this is the primary result for people who choose that course. Those sexually involved with extramarital partners do report increased sexual pleasure. So, beyond recognizing that the traditional position of fidelity is heavily value-laden as defined by social codes and religious teachings, why would a couple choose to make sexual pleasure occur only within marriage? Are there some benefits for those making this choice? For those who have had trouble solving sexual problems within marriage, there may seem to be little reward in choosing to limit sexual pleasure to a marriage. When a couple have a happy, satisfying sex life together, however, they can see many advantages in fidelity.

We have already stressed that sexual pleasure is contingent on freely chosen participation by each person. Having a choice and voluntarily exercising it are the foundation of sexual excitement. The same conditions help us realize the advantages of fidelity. Having freely chosen to remain with our partner, we find that achieving sexual pleasure with him or her is a fascinating, rewarding, and successful effort. It is when one or both partners fail to participate freely that strategies are developed to get more pleasure, very often resulting in less.

As a result of having created a living and vibrant sexual interaction, a couple experience other fringe benefits. Both within a menstrual cycle and over a period of years, partners who experience only each other can develop a sensitivity to the subtle changes brought about by time and biological rhythm. Instead of having to repeat identical sexual experiences, a couple can find within themselves a natural capacity for variation. This variation is different than that achieved by applying new techniques learned from a manual or trying a new partner. We can find within us the ability to bring out the most subtle of feelings, the most delicate stirrings, the most tender beginnings of awareness. Besides finding the pleasure available in any sexual encounter, a couple—committed to each other—make application of their sexual interaction in an eminently private and personal way. They discover that sex is a source of increased awareness of themselves and the other. This

Table 2

SIGNS OF DIFFICULTY AND SUGGESTED SOLUTIONS

Elements of Sexual Communication	Common Symptoms	Possible Solutions
Emotional Bond and Communicating Desire	1. Failure to talk openly with each other.	1. Increase each person's ability to self-disclose feelings.
	2. Repeated lack of orgasm by female.	2. Spend increased positive time alone together.
	3. Tension and lack of relaxation.	3. Avoid threatening to dissolve the marriage.
	4. One demanding the other to perform.	4. Check for angry conflict and reduce if possible.
	5. Excessive shyness or embarrassment.	
	6. Hurried and ungentle performance.	
	7. Absence of frequent touching, embracing, and exchanges of intimacy.	
Sexual Responsibility	1. Only one person initiating.	1. Review training and education about sex to see if cultural training has disparaged positive sexual expression.
	2. Excessive modesty that restricts full expression.	
	3. Failure to freely consent or refuse invitations.	2. Discuss how previous experience and early training may affect each person.
	4. Blaming each other for sexual failure.	3. Examine current relationship to see if excessive dominance is present.
	5. Double standard for males or for females.	4. Reduce criticism each may have for the other.
	6. Existence of beliefs that males and females differ sharply about feelings.	

7. Insistence by one on exceeding the desired sexual limits of the other.

8. Feeling of pressure to perform by either or both.

5. Seek professional help for the purpose of helping each feel accepting of sexual desires and asserting personal responsibility.

Optimal Variation

1. Repeatedly feeling that sex has become monotonous.

2. Feeling bored by having to participate in intercourse.

3. Excessive experimentation that violates the preferences of one or both.

4. Hurried and mechanical intercourse.

5. Lack of a set of sexual preferences.

1. Discuss what each prefers, why and when.

2. Stay within the sense of propriety felt by each person unless excessively restrictive.

3. Focus on varied feeling states as opposed to variations in techniques.

4. Acquire additional information about sexual techniques.

Physical Performance

1. Existence of physical dysfunction:

   a) impotence,

   b) premature ejaculation,

   c) retarded ejaculation,

   d) failure to be orgastic,

   e) vaginismus,

   f) sensation of pain.

1. Seek competent professional help.

2. Examine each person's individual life or relationship for sources of tension and stress and reduce if possible.

3. Increase the amount of care, warmth, and nurturance rather than criticizing or ridiculing.

4. Evaluate and improve all elements of the sexual relationship.

adds richness to the totality of their shared lives. Each person begins to express more of his or her total personality and makes it available to the sensitive discovery of the other. Sex becomes the medium for deep understanding and sharing with another person.

In contrast, when partners seek sexual pleasure with others in limited encounters, the knowledge most frequently obtained is that related to sexual passion. While we may find this temporarily rewarding, it falls short of what is possible when sexual pleasure is combined with the fascination of discovery within an exclusive relationship.

Today, perhaps more than in the past, people seem fearful of real commitment, thinking it will lead to restriction and pain. As a result, more of us enter temporary associations and develop alternative sources of fulfillment, hedging our bets to ensure we'll get what we want. Ironically, what we do to avoid the pain of commitment prevents us from making any commitment at all, and this sets the stage for separation and conflict. Thus we end up undergoing exactly that pain which we do not want. How much better life is if we each know ourselves well enough to determine what we want and why. We can then enter a marital agreement in which each partner is sure of the full and complete commitment of the other. Under such conditions, we do not need anyone else.

CHAPTER
5
DECISION-MAKING

People marry for some reasons that are uniquely their own and for some reasons that all of us have. We generally think, in any case, that marriage will help us get certain things we hope for, as well as the nice things that come unexpectedly. Being married, however, increases the complexity of our lives, and to obtain what is hoped for we must assess all the constraints that affect us and choose to make some things more important than others. Then, having created priorities, we also need to find ways of achieving as many of our high-priority goals as we can. The happiness and success of our marriage often depends on it.

Part of the marriage dialogue, therefore, pertains to selecting goals and outlining strategies for attaining them. This process is called decision-making, and its importance is revealed both in the positive results that occur when it is conducted effectively and in the unhappiness that ensues when it is not. Good or bad, decision-making has a considerable impact on any relationship because it signals how the two people organize themselves in sharing their lives. It is the making of decisions that gives evidence of our capacity to jointly create, produce, and fulfill. Failing to constructively decide upon goals and achieve them is often interpreted as evidence that two people cannot or will not be successful together. For, if we cannot make decisions and get things done, then one or both of us may reasonably question the value of being part of the relationship.

Cooperative decision-making requires following a sequence of communicational steps, each step being preparation for the next. Both people can benefit by agreeing to follow these steps. Assuming that they honor the agreement, the resulting decisions will have greater clarity and the couple will feel greater assurance that the decisions will be carried out. One way of viewing this whole process is to consider it a bridge that includes selecting a course of action, developing commitment, and thereby achieving the objective. As is the case with all interaction, it occurs at two levels. The first level, which consists of spoken words, determines what course is selected. The second level, which consists of how people go about deciding, tends to determine the degree of commitment and consequently has a great deal to do with whether the goal is achieved. Successful deciders consider both parts crucial and work to insure that their decisions identify a desired goal *and* produce a high level of motivation to achieve it. By contrast, some couples fail to decide thoughtfully and instead, impulsively or unwisely, select something that neither partner wants but both seem forced to pursue. In other marriages, one partner tries to decide most of the time, or the couple use the strategy of each deciding separately. These approaches do not yield "good" decisions since they fail to produce a high level of motivation and commitment.

WHY MARITAL DECISIONS ARE UNIQUE

The Nature of Marital Tasks

Research related to decision-making suggests that one key element is the nature of the task to which the decision is related. If it is relatively unimportant, people act differently than when both have a vital stake in the eventual outcome. The assessment of importance is affected partly by the opinions of other people. If those who are making the decision believe others think the task is crucial, the participants give greater weight to what they decide (Collins and Geutzkow, 1964).

The tasks performed by married people are among those having the greatest impact on us as human beings. Every couple must at least determine how to survive. Most of us are further confronted with decisions about child bearing and rearing, money and resource management, religious and social activities, and interpersonal events that affect general living conditions. However they are resolved, these issues have a bearing on the quality of life for each adult and child in our families.

Besides the importance these tasks have for us as married couples, their visibility to others contributes to the pressure we feel to make good decisions. Our society assigns these tasks to individuals united in a marital agreement, and we are evaluated by the way we carry them out. All in all, then, when making marital decisions we tend to be more emotionally involved than when selecting other goals.

Decision Complexity and Criteria for Success

Many marital decisions are exceptionally complex. For instance, decisions involving money management must take into account such things as the personal style and preferences of each person, the amount of available resources, a priority system for allotting funds, some accounting procedures, and flexibility within limits. Furthermore, a number of apparently separate goals are so closely related that one will affect others and in turn be influenced by goals we choose at other times. Deciding to conceive, bear, and rear a child, for example, is by itself quite full of implications relative to the achievement of other marital goals. Thus, when we are faced with making one decision, we begin to realize that we may be selecting a goal that will require decisions in other areas as well. Eventually the selection and performance of tasks becomes so intertwined that successful management must include seeing them in a total perspective where each goal is understood as it relates to others.

Most marital decisions are made at one time to be realized at a later date. Other than the confidence a couple have in their own abilities, there often is little assurance that a particular decision is right. This is determined by the passing of time and the outcome of several events. Thus we meet and decide at time A how we will live and work out all the space, events, and relationships until time B, and only at time B are we able to finally evaluate whether the decision made at time A was right or good for us. In making this evaluation we must take into account not only whether the goal set at time A is achieved, but also whether we had a quality experience while we were in the process of achieving that goal. Few decisions can be called good ones if they made us feel miserable with each other while working toward our goal.

Some people go so far as to say that it is not especially important whether we actually achieve our marital goals. In this view, the process of selecting and working toward goals is sufficient in itself to foster positive marriage. This writer, however, believes that goal achievement is also important. Unless they achieve the goals they have set, most of the time at least, couples will not feel productive. On the other hand, no goal should be so all-important that it tyrannizes us and destroys our relationship.

The Individuals Who Decide

Because of the emotional involvement created by the personal nature of marital tasks, the value orientation of the two individuals involved is an important element in their decisions. What each believes is good or bad, right or wrong, should come into play and become part of a decision. Sometimes, because values are subjective and do not fit with hard logic, they are slighted. But neither partner will find it easy to support a value-free, rock-hard, rational decision about certain questions. So, instead of trying to keep values separate or pretend they are not important, it is better in the long run if each person can identify what is valued, why it is valued, and how it should influence a decision. Of course, matters are simplified if both husband and wife have similar values. In cases where this is not true, however, it is especially important that each partner identify his or her own values and communicate them, so they can be considered during the process of deciding.

Most of our knowledge of values has derived from the study of moral philosophy, or "ethics," and the psychology of moral reasoning. From these two sources we may obtain some insights that can help a couple pinpoint what they value and why.

Abraham Mazlow proposed that there is a hierarchy of basic human needs which governs our behavior. According to this hierarchy concept, needs having the highest priority are satisfied first, and when these are fulfilled other needs press for satisfaction. The needs Mazlow identified, in their order of potency, are: (a) *physiological needs*, including hunger and thirst; (b) *safety needs* and concern for one's security; (c) *belongingness and love*; (d) *esteem needs*, or needs for self-worth and importance; (e) *self-actualization needs*, or needs for personal growth and progress; (f) *cognitive needs*, including a desire for and appreciation of beauty. These categories of need are so broad that almost all human behavior can be described as being directed toward satisfying one or another of them. Consequently, a husband or wife can begin to understand their own values if they analyze them in terms of Mazlow's categories.

Psychological needs, however, are but one part of what shapes a person's values. The second part, *present/future orientation*, is equally important. At one extreme, a person may consider ends, objectives, or goals as all-important and feel that anything is "right" if it results in achievement of a desired outcome. Such a person will channel, restrict, or shape his or her present conduct in whatever way seems necessary to ensure that a goal will be reached. At the opposite extreme, a person may be entirely means-oriented, and will evaluate all conduct as good, bad, right, or wrong in terms of its immediate consequences, without concern for how it may contribute to attainment of a goal. Such a person tends to be more spontaneous and flexible, even appearing disorganized, while he or she focuses on making the present fulfilling and not worrying about the future.

Although few people are exclusively means-oriented or exclusively ends-oriented, in most cases a person's thinking seems to be influenced more heavily by one of these concerns than by the other. When these thought patterns are joined to Mazlow's need hierarchy, it is possible to see two different sources of individual value differences that relate to marital decisions. One is the particular needs an individual will seek to satisfy and the other is the orientation, which affects how the need is satisfied.

The most obvious and elementary task a couple faces is that of satisfying hunger and thirst (physiological needs). Both probably need the same things at the same time and so will work out a plan to fill their needs. One person, however, may seem concerned only about satisfying these needs at the present time, while the other is quite worried about events that may occur in the future. When deciding what foods to buy, in what quantity, and at what price, the first person will not be very much concerned about a budget, and may even be indulgent. The other will insist on saving and planning and choosing less expensive items in order to be prepared for some future time.

Now let us also suppose that a wife was brought up in a warm, emotionally close family, whereas her husband's early life was considerably less inviting. The wife, whose needs for love and belonging have always been satisfied, is now aware of wanting to grow personally, to learn more about the world (cognitive needs). Feeling confident and secure about herself, she proceeds to try and expand her life, and very likely her children's and husband's as well. When decision points occur, however, this may conflict with the most important need of her husband, which is to belong and feel loved.

From these examples it is possible to understand how psychological needs and value orientations can affect a couple's decisions. Since both elements are present in the lives of the two individuals making decisions, both must be used in an appropriate way. Rather than making decisions that ignore the desires and values of each person, both people should recognize that marital tasks are sufficiently personal to warrant a careful examination of each person's needs and value-orientation. The actual process of reaching a decision can then include provisions to satisfy each person's needs and value orientations insofar as possible. When approached in this way, marital decisions are likely to be more satisfactory to both partners and stand a better chance of being implemented.

REASONS FOR POOR DECISION-MAKING

Time and events of ordinary living do not permit any married couple to avoid making decisions. In truth, on many issues it is not possible to *not* decide, because if no thought is given to what is to be done, time and events make our decisions for us. Even if no catastrophe results from such "decisions by default" they must be considered less than ideal, since they reflect no efforts to deal with problems in a constructive way. Thus poor decision-making occurs in two ways—either by putting off decisions or by actively trying but still failing. To help us learn to be good deciders it is useful to examine some of the reasons behind these two kinds of decision-making failure.

One reason for postponing decisions is that many of us live with a hidden, persistent fear of planning exactly what will happen to us in the future. Also, many of us are afraid to commit ourselves to something definite without a guarantee we can get it. For, if we clearly know what we are striving for, we will also clearly know if and when we fail or succeed, whereas if no goals are set, evaluation cannot take place.

Another reason why some people avoid making decisions is their pessimistic conviction that unforeseen events are always going to intervene, upsetting the best of plans. To people with busy schedules, who seem to be frequently interrupted, this attitude may seem reasonable. But, since it leaves one at the mercy of chance events, it is essentially a counsel of despair. Many of us, by contrast, believe that we can in large part determine what happens to us—that most events do not occur merely by fate or chance. Individuals who think they can "make their own breaks" in life tend to be happier and more satisfied. They can change themselves and surrounding conditions, improve their marriages, and increase their control over things because they choose to make decisions.

As contrasted with the procrastinators, some people are poor decision-makers just because they lack sufficient skill. Too often, lack of skill leads a couple to become irritated because they try to make decisions but fail to make progress. Rather than repeat this experience, they ignore subsequent opportunities to develop good decision-making skill, seeking instead for whatever alternative will get them by. Those who wish to make good decisions, however, recognize that although they may not be as competent as possible, it is worth the struggle to learn. Once skill has been acquired through practice and some decisions have been made, most of us realize that we do not need to fear failure.

A fourth reason for failing to make good decisions is the attitude with which the problem-solving process is begun. For example, some of us begin by acting as though all situations offer but two decision alternatives, "mine" and the other person's. Entering with just two alternatives reduces the decision-making conference to a round of persuasion and defense, requiring use of the rules of logic and/or manipulation. Rather than discussing the issues or problems, one or both partners are already announcing solutions. Instead of "what shall we do," it is "we ought to buy a car, and not remodel the house." These early solutions have a ring of the absolute about them, and when they are presented first without discussion, they force a partner to feel hemmed in. He or she either agrees (and allows the spouse to "win") or announces disagreement, risking criticism for failing to support the spouse's view. Since no one wishes to "lose" all the time, most married people are quite ready to disagree, and conflict ensues.

CHARACTERISTICS OF GOOD DECISIONS

We shall have more to say about skills and attitudes a little later. First, however, let's look at some of the characteristics of good decisions. Researchers have given considerable attention to some characteristics of effective decision-making as it occurs between people (Winter and Ferrera, 1967). They write that good decisions have the following characteristics: (a) Good decisions are usually completed in an optimal amount of time, being made neither too quickly nor too slowly. (b) A couple has the ability to suspend judgment when needed or adjust and reach closure when appropriate. Some good decisions are also reached through "spontaneous agreement," in which a couple share likes and dislikes to the point that they appear to "naturally" want the same thing. However, this does not mean such a decision is reached without sufficient thought; the discussion has occurred at other times and has led both to understand each other when the decision point is reached. (c) Good decisions give both individuals an opportunity of getting what each wants, or deriving "choice fulfillment," some of the time.

Effective decision-making behavior consists in trying to reach the best decision for everyone, not competing to see whose idea is best or the most accurate. In fact, husband and wife might take it as an axiom that reaching a mutually acceptable decision is as important as being "right." A corollary to this axiom is that each person must act as if his or her ideas, as well as the opinions of the other, are valuable. For, when two independent opinions are offered and considered, it increases the likelihood that good decisions will result.

The preceding comments apply to the manner in which a decision is reached. Of importance also is the form in which the decision is stated. In this respect, a good decision has the following qualities: (a) it is *clearly stated* so that both understand what is going to be done; (b) it is *sufficiently specific* so that each believes the goal can be achieved, and (c) it has at least a general *due date*, a time by which both will know whether the goal has been attained. The inclusion of these three elements in the statement of a decision does much to ensure that the goal will, in fact, be attained.

PRINCIPLES OF EFFECTIVE DECISION-MAKING

Decision-making is a fairly complex process involving specific communication skills. In effect, the quality of the decision, the effort it takes to make the decision, and whether the decision is implemented all depend largely on a couple's ability to communicate.

The types of communication skills and attitudes that help to promote good decision-making are described below.

★ *Pacing.* This refers to a couple's ability to jointly follow a sequence, adequately completing one step before going on to the next. By successfully pacing what is talked about, a couple will avoid confusing themselves by introducing distracting or irrelevant issues. Pacing also contributes to a quality decision by ensuring that judgment is not reached too quickly or in the absence of adequate amounts of relevant information.

★ *Clarifying.* During decision-making people may not say at first what they really mean, nor do receivers always hear accurately. It is useful to have a mechanism that allows clarification of what a person says until an opinion actually represents the feelings of the speaker.

★ *Tentativeness.* Early in the total process of deciding, one or both may have firm opinions or may be quite vague about what the eventual decision should be. In either case, it helps marital decision-making to offer opinions somewhat tentatively so that too great a show of power will not evoke defense and insecurity.

★ *Integrating.* Quality decisions are frequently made up of more than a single idea. Integrating is the skill of taking two or more opinions and relating them in such a way that one broader concept is formed. Compromises, for example, are combinations of two different points of view.

The importance of each of these will become apparent in the discussion which follows.

Early in their marriage a couple cannot be expected to have a refined technique for making joint decisions. They have not yet faced many important issues that require decisions, and it takes some practice to become good at it. To improve their technique and learn to make good decisions, they will find it helpful to see decision-making as a three-stage process. If implemented correctly, this process will allow a couple to make great strides in their decision-making ability.

The Entry Stage

The entry stage, because it comes first, is often the key to whether the rest of the sequence proceeds smoothly. The purposes of the entry stage are to identify what must be decided and to formulate some alternatives. Once these two things are accomplished, the entry stage is completed and the middle stage, deliberation, can be attempted.

It may seem unnecessary to spend time identifying what needs to be decided, since in most cases that is obvious. One thing is certain, however; if a couple do not begin at the same place, it is much more difficult to have similar opinions and agreement at the end. To begin, then, one partner should state what he or she thinks needs to be decided. This can be done most effectively by describing a situation or a set of circumstances, then offering a personal opinion about what the problem is. For instance, the initiator can begin by saying, "There's a problem shaping up here that we need to do something about . . ." and then describe the situation as he or she sees it. The objective at this point is simply to see whether both can agree about the general nature of the situation. The need to buy something, move somewhere, work with a child, decide who to visit during holidays, and so forth are typical situations. Consider buying a car: "The situation is that the present car is not working well, new cars are least expensive at this time of the year, I would personally like a new one, and I want to know what you think."

Effective entry requires that these opening statements be made in a *tentative fashion*. When a tone of voice is definite, with a note of finality, most hearers react to that tone of voice rather than focusing on what needs to be decided. Being tentative means describing how things *see* rather than how they *are*, while emphasizing the possibility of other points of view. This approach will improve the chances of reaching agreement about what is to be decided. In exchanging these tentative views, partners can and should ask for clarification of comments, if this is necessary, to ensure that each fully understands the other.

After agreeing what is to be decided it is then appropriate to identify alternative goals, solutions, or courses of action. The objective here should be to examine as many alternatives as seems productive. If we begin by thinking that we need to do *either* "this" *or* "that," we are likely to make low-quality decisions. Most circumstances affecting human beings offer more than two alternatives, and spending time to identify as many as are useful will increase the likelihood of finding a good one. It will also raise each person's level of commitment, because the knowledge that a given course was selected from several possible choices usually helps us to feel more confident and satisfied.

The supposed pressure or need to make a decision sometimes pushes a couple to make hasty decisions. Agreeing to spend time searching for alternatives and generating as many as possible will slow the whole procedure enough to give both people time to think. Here are a number of suggestions that can help. First, the partners should agree that all they wish to do at this point is to *identify* the alternative goals or solutions. This means that no criticism is permitted, because criticism of one proposal may discourage the originator from bringing up another. Second, it is helpful to acknowledge each idea in a positive way. This gives reinforcement to a person for having had ideas and will stimulate the production of others. Third, it is wise to pace the conversation so that none of the alternatives is discussed at any length just yet. Detailed discussion at this point will distract the couple from generating ideas. Instead, they should continue to suggest alternatives until neither partner can think of any others. Success at the entry stage is realized when several alternatives have been identified.

The Middle Stage: Deliberation

In the middle stage of decision-making, two events occur. First, each person's preferences or desires are solicited, clarified, and discussed until each can make a definite statement about what is wanted. Second, the alternatives identified in the entry stage are evaluated in conjunction with each person's preferences to determine the advantages and disadvantages of each.

Oddly enough, in marital decision-making the preferences of the two individuals are often neglected. What each wants to do, desires, or needs often gets lost in the rush to decide something and "get it over with." Even when a preference is stated, it may be glossed over as being irrelevant to a logical solution. But common sense tells us that family members and married couples will be more satisfied when their preferences or psychological needs are sought after and incorporated into the eventual decision. Learning what each person needs and prefers is therefore a crucial part of marital decision-making. It helps both to feel they had a say in the decision, and reinforces their self-esteem because the needs of each are considered of sufficient worth to be understood and incorporated. The failure to integrate a person's preference reduces his or her investment in seeing the decision implemented and decreases the probability it will ever be carried out. For this reason, couples who find that they fail to act on a decision would do well to examine whether the preferences of one or both have been fully understood and incorporated into the decision.

Adequate time needs to be allotted for exploring which alternative each person prefers. It is not enough to ask merely, "What do you think, honey?" We are not always sure what we prefer, or we may not be able at first to state it clearly. But through patient exploration and discussion, each person should eventually be able to state, "This is what *I* would like to do . . ." The time and effort this takes are never wasted. By taking the time and showing the concern, partners communicate their conviction that the relationship is at least as important as the eventual outcome.

There is another, less obvious purpose for helping each person state a preference. Early attention to the preferences of each spouse will reveal whether there are differences or agreements before more time is spent trying to come to a decision. If a disagreement exists, both know this directly, without guessing what each thinks, so both will know that compromises may need to be made in order for a final decision to emerge. And if agreement exists, as it will much of the time, then the process of decision-making may even be able to stop at this point, because a decision will have been made. Consider, by contrast, what the effects are when neither partner states a need or a preference. Suppose that a couple are preparing to go out for the evening and the fellow says, "What would you like to do tonight?" "I don't know," says she. "Whatever you would like." Thinking it important to be sensitive, he responds by saying, "I don't care either, I would like for you to say." Doing her part to help him be the leader, she suggests, "No, really, I am happy to do whatever you say." This conversation could go on indefinitely until both were frustrated. The frustration would be avoided if either or both simply declared, "I want to . . ." Identifying and declaring what each needs will at least push the conversation in the direction of a decision.

After hearing and understanding what each person needs or prefers, the logical weighing of alternatives can begin. Here the couple together consider the advantages and disadvantages of each alternative. Not a difficult task, it consists of identifying and stating what would be good, useful, or advantageous if alternative A, B, or C were selected, then what might be harmful, unhelpful, or disadvantageous if A, B, or C were selected. This can usually be done fairly quickly, and if done well it will give added information to those making the decision.

When a couple consider possible alternatives they typically identify reasons why one should be selected over the others. Here is where each person's value orientation will be displayed. The reasons or advantages, the failings or disadvantages that a person is able to see depend on this orientation. It is usually wise, therefore, to recognize and examine what each person is communicating about his or her own values. Suppose, for instance, that a husband says, "One advantage of buying a car now is that it is least expensive at this time of year . . . Another reason is that I am really tired of driving our old car." His comments reflect a present as opposed to a future orientation. The wife, too, portrays her way of viewing things by saying, "A disadvantage of buying the car now is that our savings will be spent and we won't have anything to lean on if something unexpected happens." Her concern, apparently, is for the future and making it secure.

Regardless of each person's orientation, all advantages and disadvantages of each alternative should be listed so that an analysis can be made. At this point, the communication skill of *integrating* these elements becomes useful. Husband and wife now need to combine each person's preference with the advantages or disadvantages, then examine the value orientation suggested during the discussion of alternatives. An example of integration would be for the wife to say, "I understand that you prefer to buy a car soon and the advantages are (1) it will cost less money now, (2) we need a new car to avoid repairing the old, and (3) our family could go on a trip this summer instead of staying at home. You also seem concerned with things that happen right away rather than worrying about the future." This wife has put together the husband's preference, advantages of that alternative, and his value orientation. If the same is done for the wife, then a better decision will result.

Having learned the preferences of each person listed, the advantages and disadvantages of each alternative, and integrated both of these with a person's orientation toward the present or the future, the middle stage of decision-making is completed. Adequate skill in performing this phase will enable the couple to make a fairly easy transition into the next stage, where they actually reach a decision.

Selecting and Specifying the Decision

Selecting the alternative goal or decision is easy if one alternative seems to offer the most advantages or fewest disadvantages and satisfies the preferences of both. It may not be difficult even when preferences differ, if one alternative seems to offer a good compromise. However, making a final decision is difficult if no alternative clearly has more advantages, meets more preferences, or permits a compromise. Then, a couple will need further discussion to choose between at least two different viewpoints. When this happens, the first rule of thumb is to return to each person's preference, and let each further explain why he or she wants a particular alternative. Since the eventual decision is likely to be a personal one, it seems wise to focus on and try to resolve what each person individually wants rather than to manufacture further advantages and disadvantages.

When engaging in this discussion, it is essential to keep two things in balance—concern for each other and concern for what happens. As is suggested by Moulton and Blake (1971), both these aspects are crucial when deciding between two different points of view. Only rarely will concern for what happens be much more important than concern for one's mate. On the other hand, if the desire to make peace with a mate is too strong, the quality of the decision may be low, resulting in reduced productivity and loss of marital esteem. The following dialogue is an example of a good balance between the two.

	Husband	*Wife*
Concern for what happens	"I want a new car."	"I would rather use the money to finish the house. It really needs to be done and the house would be so much nicer. Meanwhile, we can start saving up to get a car."
	"But I have had my heart set on getting another car. This one is having problems."	"You are right. The car isn't going to last much longer."
Concern for a mate	"Well, let's see what would happen if we fixed the house up first."	"Okay, we'll need to decide what we would like to have done and then determine the cost and the time."
	"Fixing the house will probably take all the money that could be used for the car, and that still bothers me."	"That's right. So we'll need to think how long it will take to save money for the car. If it takes too long, maybe we ought to get the car rather than fix the house."

The example is probably more idealistic than the reality faced by most couples. It was conjured up to illustrate two points. One is that better decisions will emerge when concern for what happens is balanced with concern for one's mate. The other is that in marriage, evidence of concern for one's mate tends to be returned in a reciprocal way. When husband and wife carefully reconsider each alternative, showing balanced concern for what happens and for one's mate, usually one alternative will now emerge as having more advantages or fewer disadvantages and as meeting the preferences of each. Identification of this alternative signals that a decision has been reached and a goal selected. The final step—and it is an important one—is to specify clearly to each other what has been decided.

For many couples, making a decision is fairly easy; it is getting action that seems more difficult. Implementing what is decided, of course, is the expectation of any couple when they begin to decide. The nature of the decisions, though, can partly determine whether either or both partners carry out what is finally agreed upon. In our culture, physiological and safety needs usually take high priority, and decisions in these areas are most often carried out. In happy marriages, however, decisions that are directed toward meeting higher-level needs are also given importance, and the partners choose to implement these decisions as often as other kinds.

Regardless of the nature of the goal, the purpose of the final stage of decision-making will not be achieved unless a couple act to raise the probabilities that the goal will be achieved. To insure that this takes place, it is important not only to agree on one alternative but to state explicitly what that alternative is, including the acts either or both must engage in to implement it.

It is surprising how often couples fail to follow through and get confirmation of a specific agreement. Grunts, headnods, and sighs are frequently part of a repertoire of communicating agreement, but use of only these in stating agreement is quite risky, since they are not always clear. Many husbands and wives report that when they make a suggestion about something, they get a grunt or nod which, taken as agreement, means something else. This isn't known until later, when the spouse says, "When did we ever agree to that?" To avoid this kind of misunderstanding, one person should summarize what he or she thinks the decision is and then ask the other to agree or disagree.

Assuming that agreement has been clearly confirmed, it is then important to specify who is going to do what in order to implement the decision. Sometimes when a couple make a decision the last thing said is something like "Okay, honey, let's do that." At the time, both believe they know who needs to do what, but when away from each other new thoughts pour in, and what each actually does can be something different from what the other expected. Time can be lost while they get together to reclarify. It is a fairly simple procedure for one to say something like, "I think we have decided that you are going to . . . and that I will . . . Is that the way you understand it also?" When this is clearly confirmed, the decision has been fully specified. This small step of specifying the decision can increase a couple's productivity because both acknowledge that they know what the goal is and how they will proceed to attain it.

RESULTS OF GOOD DECISIONS

In making marital decisions, the issue of control between two people is brought into focus. Many people enter marriage not realizing that control and who has it is a fundamental concern that must be happily resolved for the marriage to be successful. Otherwise, one or both partners will resort to continual arguments, manipulations, sabotage, or other strategies to avoid losing control to the other person. Learning to make decisions and productively carry them out will help prevent such "power struggles" from occurring.

When decisions are made according to the principles discussed in this chapter, they show concern both for goals and for the relationship between the two partners. Thus good decisions can strengthen marital bonds by proving that "both of us care." Furthermore, well-chosen goals lead to increased productivity. When couples see they can select a course of action at time A and achieve it at time B, esteem for their marriage increases, because it has demonstrated its potential for helping get things accomplished.

One couple reported they had experienced a "bad" marriage from the very beginning, which had, at the time they sought counseling, lasted for three years. Part of their difficulty centered around the inability to make decisions. It didn't seem to matter what needed to be decided. Sex, money, vacation time, child rearing—all failed to go smoothly. In counseling, it was no different. They demonstrated an alarming lack of decision-making competence. They were in so much pain they began to consider a divorce, only they could not agree on that, either. First one, then the other would be in favor; but they could not agree. Finally, after learning the skills in decision-making, they decided that what they should do was to get a divorce. But after agreeing to this, the husband said, "Say, you know, we just made a decision. Maybe we should stay together to see if we can make more of them." As far as the author knows, they have done so.

CHAPTER
6
NEGOTIATING

The dialogue of marriage is performed by two people who are, in most cases, interesting and complex human beings. Each of us has several aspects of personality that collectively represent who we are to ourselves and what we are like to other people. Even though we may hope to know every aspect of our partners, neither person can offer all of his or her personality to the other. Each one presents and in turn sees probably half of what is available. This occurs because we mutually influence each other. One person's acts stimulate or elicit certain kinds of behavior from the other, which in turn stimulate subsequent responses, and so on like links in a chain. Each link in the stimulus-response chain is made up of an act by the husband or the wife. All that a husband is able to present to a wife is controlled by how she is able to respond. Her actions in turn are limited by the way he acts. An example of this is the chain that may be started by a husband's angry behavior, which elicits sarcasm from the wife, to which he may respond with further anger, and so on.

As time passes many different stimulus-response chains are formed, some good, some bad. These are placed end to end and linked together in various ways according to a couple's personal desires and the pressures from their environment. When most of these behavior chains fit together in organized, purposeful ways to further mutual goals, the relationship is said to be in calibration.

Consider, for example, the situation of sexual intercourse, putting children to bed in the evening, or going out together. Each involves several chains of acting and responding, linked into a sequence to achieve a given purpose. But sometimes the behavior chains of two people do not link to form purposive sequences. Under certain circumstances, the couple's actions actually seem out of control, neither person's behavior influencing the actions of the other. Marriage counselors frequently find that disorganized, undirected marital events are related to marital distress. Usually, the couples do not associate their unhappiness with the lack of calibration. Even in a relationship that has in general gone smoothly, calibration may be weakened or lost as natural growth and development brings change to each person, thus throwing unforeseen kinks into the accustomed stimulus-response chains. When this happens, couples may find they no longer seem to interact effectively toward mutual goals.

There is a process of communication, called negotiation, that has the purpose of bringing a relationship into calibration. Whereas decision-making is the act of selecting goals, negotiating is the process of settling differences over who will do what and when in order to achieve them. It is a kind of communication that permits a couple to fit their actions together where they are out of calibration. It permits two people to incorporate new growth or newly discovered personal needs into their style of interaction. It allows a couple to adapt to a world filled with changing levels of pressure, unexpected crises, and enticing activities. It is, instead of a struggle to see who wins or loses, a procedure designed to help two separate and unique individuals more satisfactorily join themselves in a positive and long-lasting union.

Two human beings and their relationships are too complex and diverse to warrant negotiating and clarifying who does what in every instance. None of us have enough time or energy. There are, however, certain situations in which some form of negotiation is useful. When couples are in conflict, and their relationship is strained to the point that neither wants to do much for the marriage, negotiation can ease the strain. And even when the relationship is generally satisfactory, negotiation may be an effective way of settling practical issues of some importance.

In this chapter we describe three kinds of potential difficulties to which negotiation may be applied. Difficulties relating to how each performs a sex role are the most common, since the very coming together of two people requires that they reach some agreement—verbally or otherwise—about their respective roles.

Another area of potential difficulties—ranging from seriously disruptive problems to minor practical issues—encompasses how time is spent and who performs various tasks. In this area a form of negotiation called quid pro quo is likely to be useful. Finally, negotiation can be applied to resolve difficulties that result when partners attempt to bring about behavior changes in each other.

Before discussing these three areas of application, it seems useful to describe some aspects of communication that are relevant to all of them. Understanding these can help provide a foundation for successfully applying the principles of negotiation.

ELEMENTS OF SUCCESSFUL MARITAL NEGOTIATION

Most of the research conducted about negotiation has not been specifically applied to marriage. But even some of the general findings suggest one important guideline. Rubin and Brown (1975) have reviewed the outcomes of many studies and formulated some hypotheses about successful bargaining and negotiating. They propose that successful outcomes depend in part on the level of confidence, esteem, and trust two people have for each other. And literature about marriage suggests that a high level of these qualities results from certain practices. For example, although in business a negotiator might withhold information in order to obtain greater gains, in marital negotiating it is advantageous to share more information rather than less. Otherwise each person may not fully understand the intentions, desires, concerns, or objections of the other. Since the marital relationship continues after negotiation, as opposed to some business settlements, it also seems important that each make an effort to communicate confidence in the other. In the hassle over who gets what, we must not neglect to tell of our support for each other and our desire to help each other obtain satisfaction.

· Basic Operating Assumptions

Successful marital negotiation requires that each person voluntarily participate. Both partners need to take part in working out a cooperative plan for getting what each wants. Attempts to threaten, coerce, or intimidate probably will be responded to by withdrawal —if not openly, then covertly in the forms of passivity and neglect. Truly voluntary participation probably depends on whether a husband and wife believe that joint outcomes are more advantageous than separate attempts to get things done. Couples can create this belief if they operate on the following assumptions: (a) Maintenance and growth of the marriage is an outcome of highest priority. If what either partner wants threatens this objective, then the other need not participate. (b) Each partner must achieve some satisfaction as a result of negotiating and each must provide some support for the other. Neither partner can be *only* satisfied or *only* supportive. (c) What each does or wants must be acceptable to the other. One cannot voluntarily participate in negotiation that will result in something undesirable or damaging.

The Effects of Time on Negotiation

Time affects negotiating efforts in two ways. If there is not enough time to deal with the issues at a given point, it is not appropriate to try and reach a settlement. There is no real way to estimate the amount of time needed because it depends on the number of things being discussed. If only one issue is in question, less time is needed than if several have to be considered. After some practice in negotiation, a couple will be able to judge fairly well the amount of time required.

On the other hand, some limitation on the time devoted to a negotiating effort is desirable, for it seems that time limits tend to push people to complete the entire procedure more rapidly than when unlimited time is available. Pruitt and Dreus (1969), in studying negotiation in general, suggested that (a) heightened time pressure increases motivation to reach agreement, and (b) toughness, which requires time, diminishes as time pressure increases. The results of their study support both hypotheses. Assuming these results apply to marriage, it is advisable for couples to agree on time limits as negotiation begins.

Communication Factors

Negotiation is a situation within which accurate communication is essential. Communication effectiveness decreases when aloofness, threat, or suspicion are present. The manner in which the participants conduct themselves is also important. A stiff posture, avoidance of eye contact, slouching and inattentiveness, speech that is too rapid and crisp, and frequent interrupting have been shown to decrease the effectiveness of bargaining in experimental situations.

An important influence also is the structure given to the process. Findings from experiments conducted by Loomis (1959) and Rodlow and Weidner (1966) suggest that structuring of negotiation enhances the effectiveness of bargaining as measured by increased gain for both parties. When two people structure their interaction they agree that certain things will occur at certain times. They agree, in effect, to follow a series of stages, which are in turn also structured so that a specific purpose is accomplished in each.

As two people enter situations where negotiation is appropriate, it is well to remember that many different aspects of communication may influence the outcome. When each person appears involved, cooperative, and conciliatory, the results tend to be more beneficial for both. Note, however, that the absence of negative communication, such as threat and coercion, is not the same thing as the presence of positive behavior. Each person needs to perform positive acts of cooperation in order to maximize the chances of success.

NEGOTIATION OF SEX-ROLE PERFORMANCE

As a result of our experiences in growing up, each of us acquires a set of personal behavior patterns that fit into our concept of being a man or a woman—in other words, we learn the behaviors that constitute a sex role as we perceive it. To some people, for example, earning a living for a family is the task of males more than of females, whereas to others it does not seem appropriate to make any such distinction. Another feature of learned sex roles is the set of behaviors reserved especially for heterosexual interaction. Men learn to act somewhat differently toward women than toward other men, and women likewise acquire attitudes and actions especially for their association with males.

In marriage, both partners continue to act out their roles as learned in growing up. To the extent that each person's behavior fulfills the other's expectations and simultaneously permits each to perform his or her own role, satisfaction tends to exist. Often, however, partners find that in some respect one or the other person's role performance does not turn out exactly as expected. Where large unresolved differences exist, divorce often results. In the case of smaller disconfirmation, couples may try to adjust and, if they fail, may decide it is simply something they "have to get used to."

Actually, it is not reasonable to expect that two people are always going to act in accordance with each other's expectations. As two different individuals they will have the uniquenesses that characterize all of us. But discrepancies that begin as small differences may become major sources of unhappiness, as the following example shows.

> Connie complained that her husband, Jim, did not talk
> enough. He was one who worked, read the paper, watched
> television in the evenings, and only occasionally played with
> the children and conversed with her. She felt he did not care
> for her and reported that she was becoming increasingly
> bitter and distant. When asked if he wanted some change
> from her similar to what she wanted from him, Jim replied,

"I don't like to hassle, and I'm afraid if I tell her what I want she will argue, and then what will we have?"

In this example, the husband perceived and played his role in a way that did not fit his wife's expectations. Ignoring the situation made matters worse, until neither could talk constructively about it. The wife complained and the husband remained silent.

Rarely do a couple devote much advance thought to how their roles will mesh in marriage. Two people date, court, and marry partly because there is already some compatibility between their ways of performing roles. Then, usually without discussion, a man acts to perform a task and thereafter both he and his wife think of this task as his. The woman also performs tasks, and because of the precedent, both begin to see these tasks as her responsibility. Other tasks are performed by whoever is available, so that an interchange develops between the two. But so far, there is little if any planning of who does what and when. There has been only an implicit negotiation of how each will play the roles which were taught from earliest childhood.

This lack of planfulness can sooner or later lead to problems, as external crises or pressure push one person to silently modify his or her role, forcing an adjustment in the other person. While all of us are affected by these, a couple who have slipped into their roles without discussion are less capable of adjusting smoothly. Suppose a person comes home tired and lies down before dinner instead of giving help that is usually part of a role performance. Seeing this, the partner tries to give comfort and attention. If this is sufficiently reinforcing, we could expect an increased frequency of coming home tired, lying down, and receiving comfort. Considerable time can pass before the spouse says, "Why don't you help me like you used to?" Very simple things can thus precipitate dramatic, discomforting shifts in the way couples act when they have only an implicit form of role negotiation.

Frequently, the lack of explicit understanding of sex roles is associated with a disparity in the perceptions husband and wife have of each other. In this connection, Laing et al. (1966) developed a test to measure how closely these perceptions agreed at each of three levels. These levels for the female were: (a) what I think about him, (b) what I think he thinks about me, and (c) what I think he thinks I think about him. We shall be discussing this "perceptual spiral" in more detail in Chapter 7. Here we need only note the findings, which were that in marriages where couples were more satisfied, more perceptual agreement existed, and in unhappy or "disturbed" marriages, less perceptual agreement existed. In the author's words:

> The disturbed group are . . . much less sure of themselves and of each other at all levels. They are more in disagreement, have more misunderstanding, and in knowing they are misunderstood are liable to be incorrect as to specific issues in which they are in fact understood or misunderstood. (p. 108)

The study also supports the idea that interpersonal behavior (conjoint role performance of husband and wife) is one of the determining influences upon perception and agreement. This suggests that to be happy, couples should openly discuss and reach an understanding of the way each performs marital roles. This can be done by periodically evaluating why each performs a certain way, how important a task may be to each, and what is preferred by both. Planning to have conversations of this type will keep communication open and permit changes to occur if and when one or both prefer to alter what they are doing.

NEGOTIATING AS QUID PRO QUO

Lederer and Jackson (1968) wrote that the basis of every negotiation is a reciprocal giving of something for something received. Hence the term *quid pro quo*, meaning "something for something." Specifically, as used here, it means something of value given for something of identical value in return.

A prominent exchange theorist, George Homans (1958), wrote about social behavior in a way that is similar to Lederer and Jackson's description of quid pro quo in marriage.

> Social behavior is an exchange of goods, material goods but also non-material ones, such as the symbols of approval or prestige. Persons that give much to others try to get much from them, and persons that get much from others are under pressure to give much to them. (p. 457)

Homans further wrote that the social exchanges given and received differ according to the length of relationships. When relationships continue indefinitely, as does marriage, imbalance can easily be created. This is why an equal something-for-something basis ensures an appropriate balance or calibration of behavior.

The concept of quid pro quo may seem to be a sterile, unnatural, even mechanical approach to marriage life. Some people, at first impression, are even offended by the idea. They think that if something is given at all, it must be done without any strings attached, that it is a sign of social graciousness and a demonstration of love to give without expecting anything in return. By the same token, all of us *want* to be given to, but we are afraid to tamper with a partner's giving; it seems that if we ask for something, this infringes on the partner's freedom to offer it, and some of the value of what is given rests in its being freely offered, rather than being part of some deal.

This thinking is certainly accurate and appropriate when the things exchanged are bits of interpersonal behavior such as love, tenderness, gentleness, and attention. But there are nevertheless at least two instances where quid pro quo is an excellent basis for negotiation. One is the situation in which very severe marital discord exists. The other is when couples are attempting to decide how to allot the time they spend together.

Quid pro quo is useful in solving marital discord because of some results it produces. First, it allows couples to start their "reciprocal motors" and reestablish a basis for their relationship. This was true of a separated couple whose very first quid pro quo was two hours of babysitting by the husband in return for one home-cooked meal a week by the wife. Second, it evidences some commitment to the relationship and can thus help reduce the fear both may have that the other is indifferent. Third, in a climate of distrust and suspicion, this form of negotiation allows disclosure of what will make each happy without creating a basis for rejection. Lastly, something-for-something negotiation can act to raise self-esteem because each person justifiably earns what is received and is not obligated nor vulnerable to exploitation.

In more harmonious marriages, quid pro quo negotiation can also be advantageous. Couples usually have only a certain amount of time to be together and yet both have personal preferences about what is done during the time. If preferences conflict, they can be resolved by dividing the time, or by using one time period for one person's preferred activity and using a subsequent time for the other person's. In this way both can communicate the value of being together and at the same time satisfy each individual.

Quid Pro Quo Steps

Fortunately, the process of establishing a quid pro quo is not difficult to learn. The steps in the process do, however, require some practice before couples become proficient. These steps are described in the following paragraphs.

Structuring the Sequence. This includes identifying each of the steps that is to follow, describing what should be discussed in each step, and setting a time limit for completion of the entire process. Successfully outlining the structure will promote effective use of time, clarify communication, and lead to more specific settlements.

Identifying the Issues. This step often is difficult to complete because it requires suspension of blaming and criticism at the same time as it requires each person to identify what he or she wants. If negotiation is being used to resolve discord, each person will want something from the other. If it is being applied to resolving how to spend time together, each partner will want to do something that requires an adjustment from the other.

Bargaining. During this step both people state what they are willing to give, how often, and how much. This is more efficiently accomplished if both will say, "I am willing to . . . ," rather than asking, "What will you give?" Declaring what one is willing to do eases the strain that might be present.

Verbally Agreeing. After bargaining has been completed, the couple check to be sure that each gives and receives something, and that the things given and received are of approximately equal value. Assuming these criteria are satisfied, one person states exactly what the settlement consists of, and agreement is confirmed by the other.

NEGOTIATING A CHANGE OF BEHAVIOR

Extended involvement with another person increases the chances that each will identify some behavior in the other that is irritating or unconstructive. In order to bring a relationship into better calibration some of these actions will eventually need modifying. It is also likely that growth in one person will be manifest in his or her behavior and this too will require some adjustment.

In negotiating behavior change, a couple must first learn to eliminate distractors. A distractor is any behavioral event that by its presence provokes negative responses—for example, criticism, ridicule, nagging, autocratically ordering a change, or attempting to manipulate through temper tantrums, withdrawal, or rejection. As most people soon learn, these methods have a dismaying tendency to keep unwanted behavior around. Because of the stimulus-response nature of the interaction, they seldom or never accomplish their purpose. Instead of getting rid of undesirable acts, they become bonded to that behavior and are incorporated into the couple's interaction style. Eventually they may become the very basis of the relationship! Thus *negotiating a change of behavior will be more successful if attempts by one to change the behavior of the other do not include distractors.*

Because marriage is an intense emotional experience, the bonding of the wife's and husband's behavior is usually accompanied by repetition and emotional investment. Both of these conditions serve to tighten their stimulus-response chains. So inter-woven is the couple's behavior after a few years that one very often cannot change without a correlating change in the other. This leads us to state as a second principle that *changing behavior through negotiation will be more successful if modifications in one person's actions are accompanied by change in the behavior of the other.*

With these two principles in mind, let us now look at the steps in the process of negotiating a change of behavior.

Affirming Loyalty to the Marriage

As a first step, because high levels of confidence, esteem, and trust improve the chances of success, both people need to communicate or affirm loyalty to their relationship. Such affirmation need not be stilted or preplanned. Willingness to participate implies loyalty in itself, and no other communication may be necessary. But if a climate of suspicion and threat exists, trust needs to be expressed before there is any point in continuing.

To reduce the threat that may seem inherent in the situation, it is helpful to review the basic operating assumptions we listed early in this chapter. These may need to be restated and discussed until it is agreed that the primary purpose for asking for a be-havior change is because each wants to improve the marriage. The purpose of change is not to punish or belittle the partner.

Assessment and Clarification of Needs

This step is designed to identify a wanted change in terms of what each person needs from the other. When a husband, for ex-ample, says, "I want you to be more affectionate," he is indicating his involvement in the relationship and need for his wife.

Learning to state one's wants is not always easy. Most of us know what we "should do," what is "supposed to be done," or what "ought" to happen; but what we "want" may be different and more difficult to identify. It requires some sophisticated self-understanding to discover needs that are based on the knowledge of what is best for us.

A mistake to avoid is pointing out or describing what we *don't* want. If one partner says, "You always criticize things I do," only rarely will the spouse say, "You are right, dear." Instead, he or she will launch a defensive counterattack. A better approach would be to say, for example, "I want support and encouragement." Stating what *is* wanted is less likely to provoke defensiveness and therefore leads to more constructive work.

A request for something that does not presently exist will typically produce one of three responses. First, many people seem to feel a compelling need to explain why things now are the way they are. Thus if the husband says, "I want you to be pleasant when I come home," the wife may respond by giving an *explanation*, such as, "I don't feel very happy hassling the kids all day." A second common response is *agreement*, and a third is *direct disagreement*, *defensiveness*, or *rejection* of the idea.

Suppose person A makes a request of person B, who responds by explaining. After the explanation, person A needs to *clarify* what person B has said, rather than simply reacting to it. Thus if a husband has asked his wife to be more pleasant, it is up to him to clarify his wife's explanation of why she is not. He could say, for example, "So you are saying that you can't be pleasant after your work day." Such a clarifying statement accomplishes two things. First, it communicates the husband's willingness to listen to his wife instead of subjecting her to criticism. Second, it helps him to learn about what *she* needs. Too often, the response to an explanation is to plunge directly into additional evidence, reasons, or explanations in support of the request for a change. This is not helpful, because it tends to prompt a discussion or argument that will distract both from the point at issue. Only after clarifying person B's explanation should person A (the husband in this example) go back to the original request. He may say, "I can see it is hard for you to be pleasant at the time I come home, but I still want it if it is at all possible." By incorporating what he has learned into his restatement of what he wants, he can help prevent a distraction and increase his chances of getting what he wants without harming the relationship.

If, instead of an explanation, the husband's request is responded to by agreement, it is nevertheless important to restate what the wife has said so that both know each understands. When a request is responded to by disagreement rather than agreement or explanation, clarification is more difficult because the person who made the request may feel disappointment or anger. Rather than becoming upset at this point, however, he or she needs to calmly restate the partner's response, to be sure both understand it.

In summary, during this phase of negotiating the following things happen. First, person A states what is wanted. Second, person B gives an explanation, expresses agreement, or responds by disagreeing with or rejecting the request. Third, person A clarifies whatever response is given. Following this, the next phase can be entered.

Achieving Conciliation

To this point, the husband in our example has stated what he wanted and has listened to and clarified his wife's explanation, agreement, or disagreement. Now he approaches a step crucial to negotiation. In a case of agreement or explanation, he needs to communicate his recognition that *he* must do something to help his wife to do what he wants. Since his own behavior is bonded somehow to hers, there is probably some way he can change his own behavior to promote a change in hers. In our example, he might say, "It sounds like in order for you to be happier when I come home, we need to find some way to take the pressure off you during the day." If the wife has given no suggestion of what she needs (as might be true in the case of agreement) the husband should ask what change in him would please her. The purpose of this statement or step is to acknowledge the connection of one person to the other, and thus achieve a feeling of conciliation. Since a wife acts the way she does in part because of the actions of her husband, and vice versa, when he suggests that both need to do something he is only reaffirming the truth.

Having determined in general what it is that both must do, the couple can then get down to the specifics of what is wanted or needed. In our example, since the husband requested a happier wife at the time he comes home, he needs to describe what that means to him. He might say, "I would like you to smile, give me a kiss, tell me about a success," or, "Don't tell me your problems right away, say something else." In return, his wife might say, "I want to be able to get ready for you. I would like to be able to get a babysitter some time during the week, so I can relax and get away."

It is important to be specific in describing what is needed. If one spouse says, "I want you to be happier when I come home," or "I need to get away from the kids," this does not help the partner to translate the request into action. Thus each partner should ask for details, to get a clear idea of what actions on his or her part will constitute a satisfactory change. Spending sufficient time at this point improves the possibility that both will get what they want.

Now, let's examine the husband's approach if his wife has flatly disagreed with and refused his request. After clarifying her response, he asks her what he can do for her. In doing so, he is not giving up his request, but is gathering information from her that he can use to get what he believes he needs. After learning what she wants, which may be something quite unrelated to whether she is pleasant when he comes home, he can then move to conciliation, saying, "Well, I can see that we need to find a way to allow you to be satisfied and for me to have a happier wife." Then, as with explanation or agreement, they identify some specific things each can do so they will realize what each wants.

Declaring What Each Will Do and When

To help couples get what they want from each other it is best to avoid phrasing the agreement in terms of "If I do this, then you have to do that." Such a trade-off may work when minor issues are involved, but when the negotiation is about behavior change it has a built-in trap. Each partner may hold off on performing his or her part, to see if the other actually comes through. No one likes to give up habitual ways of acting, so each may even secretly hope the other *won't* perform as promised. Eventually, a round of blaming and counterblaming ensues, each laying responsibility for failure of the agreement at the other's door.

Therefore—contrary to any logic of rewards and punishments, tit for tat, or holding each other accountable—a more fruitful approach is for each partner to simply declare *what he or she is willing to do,* without reference to the other's actions. The husband in our example could say, "I am willing to help arrange and pay for a babysitter to help you get some time to relax." His wife can then indicate what behavior she is willing to try when he arrives home. That is, instead of trying to get a definite commitment from the other person, each partner volunteers to do something, with no attempt either to hedge in the offer or to bargain for the change. In volunteering, each assumes responsibility for his or her own behavior only. If and when the husband and wife change their behavior as promised, it will be clear that each was motivated by a personal commitment and willingness rather than by any constraints imposed by the other. Thus "love," evidenced by freely doing things for the other, may be openly demonstrated. Constraining a partner and making commitments too explicit and tight can preclude free action and create suspicion that what is done for one happens for reasons rather than love and unselfishness.

The preceding suggestions for effective negotiation of behavior change are summarized in Table 3.

RESULTS OF SUCCESSFUL NEGOTIATION

It is deeply discouraging to persevere in a marriage that offers some good but mostly bad, and to feel that little, if anything, can be done to improve it. The chief outcome of successful negotiation is the

Table 3

SUMMARY OF NEGOTIATING FOR BEHAVIOR CHANGE

Step 1. *Affirming Loyalty to the Marriage*

Both partners express their commitment to each other and agree to avoid distractors; they then move to Step 2.

Step 2. *Assessment and Clarification of Needs*

After person A states what is wanted, person B can give three possible responses:

a) Person B *agrees* to person A's requests; person A clarifies what person B has said and moves to Step 3.

b) Person B *explains* why things are the way they are; person A clarifies what person B has said and restates the original request, then moves to Step 3.

c) Person B *rejects* person A's request; person A clarifies what person B has said and moves to Step 3.

Step 3. *Achieving Conciliation*

Depending on what has happened in Step 2, conciliation is initiated by person A as follows:

For (a) agreement or (b) explanation, person A acknowledges that he or she must do something so that person B can give what person A requested.

For (c) rejection, person A communicates that a way needs to be found so that both person A and person B can get something they want.

Movement to Step 4 occurs when both persons have identified some specific things each wants the other to do.

Step 4. *Declaring What Each Will Do and When*

Avoiding trade-offs, coercion, threats, rewards, or punishments, person A states what he or she is willing to do and when, then listens to or asks person B what he or she is willing to do and when.

confidence that things can be changed, problems can be worked out, and gradual improvement will appear. Aside from direct benefits that each gains from the agreement that emerges, successful negotiation allows both persons to observe themselves in a relationship that promotes rather than retards personal growth. This increases their desire to want to be with each other, and this in turn contributes to the vitality and excitement of their marriage.

Negotiation is a communication process that enables two people to maintain a balance between being separate individuals and being marital partners. Almost all of us, at one time or another, feel the conflicting pressures that push us to sacrifice ourselves for the marriage or urge us to retain our separateness. Back and forth, in and out we go, sometimes with little direction. If we learn to negotiate, however, we can seek personal fulfillment and at the same time be responsible partners in a marriage relationship.

CHAPTER
7
METACOMMUNICATING: TALKING ABOUT HOW YOU TALK

According to the authors of *Pragmatics of Human Communication* (Watzlawick, Beavin, and Jackson, 1967), fully 85% of the time, in a family or marriage, the message a sender sends is not the same message the receiver receives. Although this figure may seem surprisingly high, the presence of miscommunication is well known to almost every married couple. Most husbands and wives have experienced the frustration of not being able to "get through," thinking they are saying things clearly but finding that the other doesn't understand.

Communication between humans at any time may be unclear. In marriage, some conditions exist which increase the probability that messages will be misunderstood. Oddly enough, marriage can also be a relationship in which two people develop a special code that they use with precise understanding. In general, however, we could all improve our communication by discovering what we do to distort either what is sent or received.

WHY MESSAGES BECOME DISTORTED

A major reason for inaccurate communication is one we have already touched on in earlier chapters—the fact that any sender sends more than one message at a time. In fact, several messages are simultaneously transmitted to the receiver. The topic or content —what people talk about—is only one. The topic may be a person's feelings or internal experience, both people's interpersonal experiences, or extrapersonal subjects which are fairly abstract and do not involve people at all. But while the speaker is talking verbally about something, other messages which are nonverbal are being sent as well. Voice tone, facial expression, gestures, posture, manner of dress, and/or body movements also convey messages to a receiver. According to Merhabian (1972) these media of communication actually account for more than 90% of what a receiver picks up from the sender! This means that the words people say are much less important in some respects than the observed nonverbal behavior.

If the existence of multiple messages were the only reason for miscommunicating, some messages would be accurately sent and received. Suppose a person simultaneously sent the following messages: (a) "I am talking about cars." (b) "I am tired or bored." (c) "My back hurts." (d) "I would rather be talking with someone else." If a receiver tuned in to at least half of these, some communication would be taking place.

Accurate communication is made more difficult, however, because the multiple messages are not separate or independent. Instead, they are of different logical orders, and the higher levels tell the receiver what to do about the lower levels. Figure 3 displays how this works.

Level I, the lowest logical order, consists of the actual meanings of the words. Level II is of a higher logical order because any of the nonverbal behaviors shown is more general than the meaning of any series of words. Several different arrangements of words can convey the same meaning, given appropriate nonverbal behaviors. A difference in nonverbal behaviors, however, can drastically alter the meaning of a single statement. Sarcasm is a good exam-

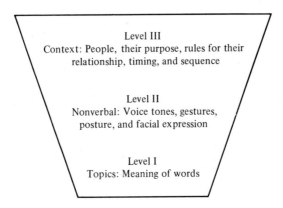

Figure 3
The logical levels of marital communication.

ple. When words with a positive meaning are said in a certain tone of voice and with strategic hesitations, this tells a receiver to take the opposite meaning. This reversal of meaning is a general effect, occurring when any positive series of words is spoken with the appropriate voice tone.

Level III, the context, is the highest logical level because it subsumes the first two. Word meanings and nonverbal behavior both occur within a context that includes people, the rules for their relationship, and the time and purpose of the people's interaction. Just as Level II tells a receiver how to interpret Level I, the context at Level III simultaneously tells him or her how to interpret both Levels II and I. Loud laughter, funny jokes, and exaggerated gestures in the context of a party mean something quite different from what the same behavior means during a funeral. The context has determined the meaning of verbal and nonverbal behavior. Poor communication may therefore result from misinterpretation at any of three levels—in hearing the words, in observing the nonverbal behavior, or in recognizing the context (Satir, 1967).

Another complication that can arise in communication is *sequence distortion*—an obscuring of messages that may result from the nature of the two-person context. Since two people cannot effectively talk at exactly the same time, one person speaks at time 1 (statement A_1), the other person responds at time 2 (statement B_1), the first person makes further comment at time 3 (statement A_2), and so on. This sequence means that when a wife makes a statement (A_1) to her husband and he responds (B_1), her next statement (A_2) should relate both to her first comment and to her husband's response. This is the point at which sequence distortion can occur, for suppose person B's response to a statement made by A does not logically or emotionally relate to it. Then statement A_2 cannot logically be consistent with both statements A_1 and B_1.

For example, a wife angrily says to her husband (A_1), "I simply cannot stand being alone all the time." And her husband responds rationally (B_1), "All wives get frustrated some of the time." To which of these should the wife reply? To her own previous statement—which would be more effective—or to her husband's response? She could follow up on her first statement, ignoring her husband, and say, "I want you and me to do something about it," or she could ignore her first statement and respond to her husband's by saying, "I don't think all women are frustrated, one of my friends isn't." If she has to make a choice between these comments at time 3, then she will have to ignore one of the previous two comments, and accurate, complete communication will not take place.

A more complex example of sequence distortion was viewed by the author when a couple requesting help with their son came for their first joint counseling session. The father, mother, and son attended. When interviewed previously, the parents had described the boy as, "A good boy, but he feels worthless and is not motivated. He also fails at things he wants to do." The father had appeared pleasant and easy-going, but there was one quirk in his conversation. He often qualified things he said by adding, "But on the other hand . . ." The mother was fairly quiet but extremely positive. The son reported he had achieved many things in his life but he also said, and apparently believed, many disparaging things about himself—for example, "I fail at everything I do," or "No girl will ever want me." When the three people were brought together, it seemed that whenever the son said something good about himself (which rarely occurred) the mother was either noncommittal or silent. The father, however, invariably qualified his son's positive statement. Thus if the boy said, "I believe I have done the best I could," the mother was silent and the father would reply, "But on the other hand, there are some things you could have done better." The son would then say, "Oh, yes, I guess that is true," and then talk about his failings.

So far, when the son would make a positive statement (A_1) the mother was silent (B_1), and the father qualified it (C_1). The son, at A_2, could then respond to A_1 (his original statement) or to B_1 or C_1 (his mother's and father's responses). Since his mother's response was ambiguous, he followed the father's lead and reversed his original opinion. Instead of being consistent with A_1, the boy responded to C_1. Thus, through sequence distortion, communication failed, for the son thought the father disapproved of him, whereas the father was only trying to help the boy avoid taking an absolute and definite stand.

At the emotional level, the sequences of conversation between husband and wife present another potential barrier to effective communication. While one person's actions are being woven into a sequence with the other's, emotions are also exchanged between the two people. After a time, certain patterns of emotional exchange emerge, so that when a given feeling is displayed by one person it tends to call forth a particular emotion in the other. These two emotions are then said to be *bonded*. If emotional bondings are pleasant and predictable they usually contribute to good communication. For instance, if display of a loving or romantic feeling is bonded with a similar response in the partner, both tend to enjoy and perceive each other's messages fairly accurately. It may happen, however, that in the course of living together several of one person's feelings become bonded to dissimilar feelings in the other. Whenever this *discrepant bonding* occurs, poor communication and frustration result. Many couples, for example, find themselves in a situation described by one husband.

*We never seem to be able to get together. When I want to be
affectionate she either rejects me or laughs. When one of
us wants to talk seriously the other avoids it or treats it
lightly. The only time we feel the same way is when we are
mad.*

Counselors of troubled married people can attest that discrepant bonding is a common problem. If one person frequently experiences and expresses one emotion at the same time as the partner expresses something discrepant, both partners begin to believe
that love has died and that they are staying together out of some
necessity, or even to fight. Believing we are quite different from
one another is all right if we also know there are commonalities.
But if we do not think we share much similarity with the person we
marry, then we have some grounds for fearing we are not understood, valued, or loved.

The roots of discrepant emotional bonding are most often the
failure, early in marriage, to clear up inaccurate communication
such as that which may arise from multiple messages or sequence
distortion. When messages are not clear, it is easy to see how two
people may simultaneously develop two very different sets of feelings. If a couple cannot discover what is causing the miscommunication and talk about the reasons for each person's feelings, the
feelings remain as originally experienced, and repeated exchanges
merely reinforce the discrepancies. The slow drift apart has begun.

If the clarity of messages is ever to be improved, then rather
than leaving communication to happenstance, a couple must find a
way of correcting the poor and encouraging the good. Rather than
continue to misunderstand and so hurt each other, they need to
discover some mechanism or method that identifies the areas of inaccurate communication and enables the couple to change. Such a
method is provided in the form of communication called *metacommunication*. Meta means "about." When a couple metacommunicate they are talking *about* how they talk, as a means of improving their communication.

One or all of four things can be discussed when we metacommunicate. (a) We can clarify the literal meaning of words spoken

so that correct understanding occurs. (Example: "I didn't understand what you just said.") (b) We can discuss how the nonverbal behavior and context (the higher logical levels) relate to what is talked about. (Example: "When you told me about your pay increase, why were you frowning?") (c) We can talk about the sequence and clear up inaccuracies due to sequence distinction. (Example: "I didn't understand what you said at first, and you didn't understand what I said in response to your first comment.") (d) We can discuss each person's feelings so that each discloses what is felt and why.

WHY METACOMMUNICATION IMPROVES COMMUNICATION

People working together in any organized way cannot improve themselves and their joint performance if they do not interrupt their normal operations periodically and evaluate what they are doing. The more effective business organizations, in fact, make evaluation a standard procedure. Marriage, as a continuous relationship, also needs to provide periods in which the couple pause in the regular flow of living and examine together whether they are as happy as they could be. Some couples carry this to extremes—at regular intervals they stop all else and worriedly analyze the very basis of their relationship. Such "agonizing reappraisals" are not what we are recommending here. Instead, we are referring to the sharing of observations and information to supply *feedback*.

Feedback, a term that originated in cybernetics and systems theory, is any information about results that can be used to help make corrections and adjustments in an ongoing process. In interpersonal exchanges, for example, one person's responses to the other's acts constitute a type of feedback. That is, if one tells a joke and the other doesn't laugh, then the joke teller has received feedback that either the joke or the manner of telling was not funny. As applied to metacommunication, feedback is obtained when a couple examine events that have occurred between them and share what each has observed. On the basis of this information exchange they can then decide what adjustments or corrections in their interaction may be helpful.

Unfortunately, many people are reared in circumstances that do not permit cooperative examination of a relationship. As children, they are not permitted to discuss the parent-child relationship with their parents. As students, they are not often invited or allowed to evaluate the teacher-student relationship. The only models they have for adult roles seem inflexible in their views. Thus, although they withhold their feelings and ideas while growing up, such people tend to hold rigidly to their opinions as adults. Instead of being able to comprehend that two adults may hold different opinions, a person with this conditioning assumes that if "I" think it, then it must be so, and no amount of conversation will help him or her to see things from the viewpoint of another.

When a person feels bound to hold rigidly to one opinion, however, he or she also tends to be insecure and to see or read personal threat into anyone's attempts to provide feedback. When a husband or wife tries to share an observation, this anxious reaction may reveal itself as extreme defensiveness, intense anger, or withdrawal. To complete the cycle, this person tends also to reject efforts by subordinates (children, students, employees) to discuss relationship issues. Ironically, he or she frequently feels lonely and hurt but does not understand why this is so or what to do about it. This very circumstance is almost invariably associated with the discrepant emotional bonding that we described earlier.

When people have the ability to consider at least two viewpoints, their task in marriage is much easier. Instead of feeling tension and apprehension, each person can offer an opinion, listen to that shared by a partner, and consider both viewpoints worthy. Practicing metacommunication promotes objectivity, helping us to see ourselves as another may see us. It also makes it easier to accept the possibility that two points of view may exist, and thus helps us become more flexible.

When we become open to another person's view of our personal experience, we become aware that our perceptions of each other exist in what is called the *perceptual spiral*. Because there are two people involved, and each person can not only think but also think about what the other thinks, each person's perception of the other exists on three connected levels. What literature exists about the spiral of perception suggests that successful marriages are those in which more understanding exists in the way each perceives the other at each level.

The spiral of perception and how it operates for married people have been described by Watzlawick, Beavin, and Jackson (1967) and Laing, Phillipson, and Lee (1966). These authors use different terms but the similarity in what they describe is quite apparent. According to Watzlawick et al., the levels of the spiral are:

1. How I see you, how you see me.

2. How I see you seeing me.

3. How I see you seeing me, seeing you.

An example given by Laing et al., makes the spiral clearer. If X stands for any issue, it is possible to distinguish:

1. The husband's view of X.   First level

2. The husband's view of his
   wife's view of X.   Second level

3. The husband's view of the
   wife's view of his view of X.   Third level

Keep in mind that a parallel situation exists for the wife. To see how this works in more detail, suppose a wife is thinking about whether she and her husband love each other. At the first level she considers, "Do I love him?" Then, going up the spiral, she could ask herself, "I wonder if he thinks I love him?" Going further to the third level she asks, "I wonder if he thinks I think I love him?" With the husband asking the same questions we have the possibility that their perceptions will agree or disagree on three levels. This is illustrated for the wife as follows:

Wife	*Husband*	*Result*
1. I love him.	She loves me.	Agreement
2. Does he know I love him?	I know my wife loves me.	Agreement and understanding
3. I wonder if he thinks I think I love him.	If someone asked my wife if she loved me, she would say yes.	Agreement and understanding

For most of us there is an increase in confidence and fulfillment when we believe that our own view matches that of the other person. If our perceptions match but we do not know they do, or if they do not match and we cannot resolve the difference, then we live alienated from one another. Metacommunication is a way to learn whether we agree, and if we do not, to resolve the disagreement.

In summary, metacommunication is a valuable kind of communicating because (a) it provides feedback by which to make adjustments in the ongoing interaction between two people, (b) it helps prevent discrepant emotional bonding by clearing up inaccuracies in communication, and (c) it promotes confidence by giving two people a way of verifying their mutual perceptions of each other.

METACOMMUNICATION TECHNIQUES

Rather than being a single technique, metacommunication encompasses a variety of techniques. Most couples metacommunicate in some way, even if it is only during the making-up time following a quarrel. Statements like, "I thought you meant..." or "Didn't you say..." are metacommunicative. There are dozens of other types of metacommunication and it is not the purpose of this section to list them all. Rather, we shall make some general comments that apply to various ways of metacommunicating.

Scheduling Times for Metacommunication

For some couples the only time that metacommunication occurs is after a problem has arisen. Time and again, they go through a disruption caused by poor communication and then talk closely. Since making up constitutes a positive experience, a husband and wife can inadvertently learn to fight in order to have the fun of talking and making up. This approach has real risks attached, because the behavior of both can escalate to the point where the number of fights increases and making up decreases. Rather than allow this to happen, it is wise to begin to metacommunicate as a means of prevention and maintenance. A person does not have to have negative feelings to do so. Talking about good as well as things that need improving will prevent much conflict and create a more open atmosphere for subsequent conversations.

Like other forms of communication, metacommunication begins with a signal or cue of some kind so that both know what is to follow. While the process is being learned, it is useful to make the initiation very definite and observable. And it is helpful to set a regular time in which to talk. This regular time does not mean metacommunicating cannot also be done spontaneously. But if it is not scheduled at the outset, we have a tendency to forget about doing it altogether, because unless there is open conflict it is easy to assume that full agreement and understanding exists. This is seldom true. So, some regular sessions can be helpful as practice sessions.

Starting can be done with the announcement by one partner that he or she would like to talk about some aspect of their communication. "I have something I want to talk about, when is a good time for you?" As with any other interaction that is taken seriously, sufficient time needs to be allotted for a careful discussion. If two people are going to spend time considering several aspects of their communication, more time will be required than if they are only going to discuss one point. After some regular periods of practice in metacommunication have successfully taught both a valuable method, then they can metacommunicate any time it seems appropriate.

Describing What Is Observed

The observations shared in metacommunication may deal with events in both personal and interpersonal behavior. It is especially useful to consider things related to the logical orders of communication and to the spiral of perception. One partner may, for example, describe to the other, "You say you are happy, but you look depressed." This description contrasts two aspects of one person's behavior and asks for clarification between the first logical level (meaning of words) and the second (nonverbal behavior). Or one partner may say, "I didn't talk to you because I thought you wanted to be left alone, but I guess I was wrong." This focuses on what one person thought about the other's thoughts, and is an attempt to clarify misperception.

Good descriptions of observed behavior omit any evaluating or labeling of someone's actions. Instead, the speaker focuses on the behavior alone. "I see myself talking rather loudly," is a description. "I am a loudmouth," is a label. Most of us use labels as part of our everyday conversation, so it is difficult to talk without using such terms. But most labels carry evaluative messages, which interfere with objective discussion of the behavior in question. This is one of the most difficult things for individuals to learn when they first practice metacommunication. Another habit that interferes with objective description is the use of absolutes. Both people will benefit if they give descriptions of behavior in comparative terms—that it happens more often or less often, is more intense or less intense—rather than saying something is absolutely one thing or another. "You get more angry the longer we argue and I do the same," is a description. "You are always mad when we talk," is an absolute.

Some people get into the habit of making inferences from another's behavior which they fail to share. This interferes with good descriptions. Suppose, for example, that a husband avoids answering questions the wife asks. Possible inferences by the wife could include: (1) "He is hiding something." (2) "He feels guilty about something." (3) "He is uninvolved in our marriage." (4) "He doesn't care about me. (5) "He doesn't love me or he would not hide anything." Rather than conjecturing on the basis of limited information, the wife should include in her description of his behavior both that which she has observed and her inference about it. She may say, "I think you are hiding something when you don't answer my questions."

Finally, descriptions are generally more effective when they concern events close to the present, rather than events that go back to the distant past. Things that have happened in, say, the past week probably will be adequately remembered by both people. Beyond that, recall may be too fuzzy to be useful, and it may appear that the person describing something is doing so with the ulterior motive of getting revenge.

Disclosing Feelings

Earlier in this chapter we described the discrepant emotional bonding that results when two people fail to correctly interpret each other's feelings. Disclosure of the feelings that are associated with events that are described is therefore an important part of metacommunication. For example, a partner may say, "When you say that to me, it seems so strong I get scared and back off."

Psychologists suggest that strong feelings are usually best expressed by talking about them rather than acting them out. Telling someone of your anger, for instance, is a less threatening approach than is raising your voice, swearing, withdrawal, or stomping around. When feelings are not talked about, but are acted out instead, the receiver is unsure of what to do. When a receiver hears words *and* the tone of voice, more certainty exists. And, generally, the receiver does not think he or she needs to get angry in return since when it is verbally expressed it is clearly the sender's anger.

This point is related to the concept of *owning* provided by Perls (1969). Contrary to the belief of many people, our feelings are self-caused, and although they may arise in response to another person's actions they are not created or caused by that person. Owning means that a person says, "I feel," or "I am feeling," or "I am feeling this because you . . ." The focus is on the feeling of the person who is talking, not on the actions of another person. Owning one's feelings is an important aid to clarity in metacommunication.

Another suggestion for disclosing feelings is to keep their expression tentative. Emotions do not usually have fixed intensity, nor are they always tied to the same behavior. Therefore, while it is usually appropriate to express any feeling, the person needs to qualify what is said by recognizing that (a) "I may feel differently another time" and/or (b) "I know this intensity will probably not continue." Statements like, "I think I am feeling," or "It seems to me," show sufficient tentativeness to acknowledge the changing nature of emotions.

Relevance is another key to effective disclosure. Sometimes during metacommunication a person may describe something but disclose a feeling irrelevant to it. Suppose a wife says, "I don't think we talk to each other enough, and I am so upset about our marriage I can't stand it." Rather than focusing on the issue of "not talking," the wife's feeling-statement has broadened the conversation to include the whole marriage. The husband probably will be distracted away from the issue the wife wants to discuss. For similar reasons, it is also helpful to disclose only one feeling at a time.

If a disclosure is relevant and tentative it also needs to be personal. For example, it is quite unfair to say something like, "The children and I feel . . ." or, "We feel that you should . . ." First of all, if the receiver believes what is said then the response must be directed toward everybody included in the sender's statement, which is not usually possible. Secondly, including other people is a form of exerting pressure, and this does not contribute to a positive relationship. Thirdly, the person who includes other people is almost asking to have his or her own feelings ignored, because the hearer will tend to react to the idea that everybody feels a certain way, instead of trying to understand how the speaker feels.

Finally, risk-taking is also an essential element of disclosure. In many marital situations there are both things that need to be expressed and things that do not. Generally, those that do need expressing are related to improving the relationship, as opposed to being accusing or blaming. Not knowing clearly what is best to say, however, many people choose to say nothing in order to remain safe. As a case in point, one stoic man finally told his wife, after 32 years of marriage, that he hated pumpkin pie. She was surprised to hear this because she did not like it either, but since she thought he did, she had unselfishly gone on for years making something which neither wanted.

It is true that we run some risk of hurting or being hurt when we disclose what we feel, but, by following the guidelines previously suggested, we can reduce the risk of hurting and improve our communication. These guidelines are summarized as follows:

★ Verbal expression of feelings is more effective than acting them out.

★ Disclosure of feelings is more effective if the person *owns* the feeling, saying, "I feel," rather than projecting the feeling somewhere else.

★ It is best to be tentative in expressing the feeling.

★ To be helpful, a disclosure should be one that is relevant to a specific event.

★ The disclosure should be personal, reflecting only the speaker's feelings and not including those of other people.

Hints for Achieving Understanding

Misunderstanding is not always a disaster, but there are some times and types of conversations where it may be quite serious, and careful attention should be given to whether each person understands. When the conversation focuses on the relationship of two people, as it does during metacommunication, working to clarify and understand is essential.

In Chapter 3 we discussed at length some reasons for and methods of achieving understanding. Here we may add that during metacommunication each partner can enhance the conversation by following a few simple procedures. Talking in fairly short sentences and using words common to the vocabulary of each, for instance, will help. Increased use of clarifiers, such as "I think you mean" or "Let me see if I understand" will add more clarity. Also, demonstrating attention through head nodding, leaning toward the speaker, and eye contact will increase the desire and freedom to speak.

METACOMMUNICATING: A SUMMARY

Doing something to improve communication could probably help every marriage. All of us seem to have some areas where things run fairly smoothly and some where they do not. As a means of achieving improvement, metacommunication can be used both during planned sessions and spontaneously. Conversing in this way, by mutual agreement, can help a couple improve communication because each partner learns the impact that his or her communication behavior has on the other and how both participate in their relationship. When a husband learns what a wife has noticed and what her feelings are about the way he communicates, he is in a position to adjust his behavior in appropriate ways. The same is true for her. Furthermore, taking time to talk about how each talks to the other can promote individual growth. When a person more clearly sees the effects of his or her actions, it is easier to identify goals that will result in improvement.

All couples metacommunicate in some degree; however, to apply the ideas in this chapter, they will need to consciously increase or refine their use of metacommunication techniques. Although there are many ways of metacommunicating, the basic form is as follows. First, a couple need a definite way of announcing the beginning of metacommunication to each other. It may be as open as "I want to talk, is now a good time?" or other cues may be used. One person then describes some communication event that he or she has observed. The objective is to gain a better understanding of (a) the relationship between words and nonverbal behavior, (b) the relationship between two sets of nonverbal actions, (c) the relationship between the context (where and when something happens) and the use of words and nonverbal behavior, or (d) the relationship between levels of the perceptual spiral. Having described something, the speaker also discloses the feelings he or she experiences in connection with the event described. And throughout metacommunication, each person clarifies what the other says to insure that understanding is achieved.

Allotting time for metacommunication often means that something else must go or be put aside for a short time. In many marriages this may mean a little less television watching, reading, or other leisure activity. If the experience of many couples is any evidence, however, adjusting their schedule to metacommunicate is well worth the effort.

CHAPTER
8
TIME DRIVING

Time has largely been neglected as a factor in communication. Yet it plays a vital role. Among the ways in which it bears on the interaction between two people are the following, suggested by Kantor and Lehr (1975):

(a) *Frequency* of repeated events, including such things as, "how often people see each other, play a game, go out, or read a book."

(b) *Duration setting*, which consists of determining how long events will last. This usually is based on experience that indicates the length of time positive feelings results from doing something.

(c) *Scheduling*, or advance planning of "deadlines for the completion of goal-oriented tasks."

(d) *Monitoring*, which provides an assessment of whether the use of time is beneficial for each person involved.

(e) *Priority setting*, which consists of deciding which events are more important than others.

(f) *Programming*, or developing plans to use time as a means of achieving certain desired characteristics. For example, we may program ourselves to spend our money to enjoy things in the present as opposed to saving to prepare for some future event.

As part of an ongoing dialogue between husband and wife, use of time is probably one of the most important facets of communication. The flow of married life is punctuated by a variety of activities, each constituting a sequence of interaction that occupies a finite interval of time. Going out for the evening, getting children into bed, preparing and enjoying meals, and pursuing religious activities are all situations for which a couple develop a sequence in which each does something in order for both to succeed.

The couple's stream of communication is also punctuated by *communicational programs.* Some of these occur as couples talk about different topics such as religion, sex, politics, or in-laws. Other programs are generated when couples move from place to place or as they interact at different times of day and with other people. Usually, when one of these programs is initiated, the partners have a fairly definite sequence of acting and talking, one that may be different for a discussion about religion than it is for a conversation about in-laws. If we could examine a routine day's interaction, we would find that it was made up of a number of communicational programs linked together, most often without the couple's being aware of them.

If the outcomes of most of their communication programs are positive, things tend to go smoothly for a couple; if the outcomes are often negative, they do not. But, having been interlocked together, a couple may continue to perform negative programs even if both realize the outcome may be unhappy. They may feel like victims, routinely going through something they know will have unhappy consequences, but they still feel compelled to do so. Fortunately, because programs are learned, then repeated at definite times, it is possible to employ time itself as a means of changing the sequence and thereby improving the outcome. The method of doing so is called *time driving.*

The principle that underlies time driving was employed in a study reported by Cairns (1967). His research involved fourth grade students. They were divided into two groups whose task was to sort small cards into various groupings. Before the task was begun, the experimenter brought one group into a room and gave them the following instructions:

> In a few minutes I will request that you sort some cards. When you do it correctly I will say, "right." When you do it incorrectly, I will be silent.

The experimenter then had these students rejoin the others. Both groups then started sorting cards while the experimenter carefully acted the same way toward both. Which group performed better, and why? As might be guessed, the group who received prior instruction did a better job. The author concluded that this was because the superior group knew the meaning of the word "right" and of silence. When they did not hear this key word immediately after sorting the cards, students in the instructed group knew they were incorrect. Even though the others may have known what "right" meant, they did not know the meaning of the experimenter's silence. Consequently, these students were not able to correct themselves as rapidly as students in the instructed group.

Although this example involved students and a researcher, the principle applies also to marriage. Being able to anticipate a future situation, the researcher instructed the students at time A how to interpret his behavior at time B. Let us consider how this works in a marital situation. Suppose a couple have developed the following communication program.

> *According to the husband, "We have gotten so that when she is critical I withdraw. Then when I withdraw she complains about my lack of caring for her. When this happens I usually stop talking and go ahead and do what I want anyway."*
> *His wife probably sees this as evidence of his lack of caring, which stimulates further criticism from her.*

The husband recognizes how his actions and those of his wife are intertwined in terms of what his actions mean to her and what hers mean to him. Applying the principle illustrated in the research study, this couple could time drive by discussing at one time what meaning they should attach to each person's behavior the next time the negative situation confronts them, and by planning new behavioral sequences to replace the undesirable one. We shall discuss this procedure in some detail later in the chapter.

THE EFFECTS OF MARITAL TIME DRIVING

Time and Meaning

When Douglas MacArthur and Harry Truman disagreed about the conduct and objectives of the Korean War, they met in a historic confrontation. Both flew to an intermediate location and planned to arrive at approximately the same time. According to one account (we do not vouch for its authenticity), General MacArthur instructed his pilot to circle the airbase so that President Truman's plane would land first. This would have placed the President in the position of greeting the general when he landed. Rather than permit this, President Truman is alleged to have ordered Mac-Arthur's pilot to land, so that the President of the United States could be given due recognition.

This story illustrates how timing can shape what events mean. In this case, the person who got the other to act first was accorded higher status. Similarly, in marriage the timing can affect the meaning of actions. The person who speaks first, speaks more often, gives advice, or offers more suggestions generally is perceived as being more powerful than the one who only responds, reacts, and replies. Whether a husband or wife is viewed as more influential may thus depend on how often he or she starts events in which both participate.

Within a marital relationship the timing of a person's actions is related to loving. For instance, the individual who believes she or he does all the initiating may come to the conclusion that the other person does not care or lacks commitment. If a husband is nearly always the one who starts sex, he may begin to wonder if his wife really wants it or if she participates out of a sense of duty.

Since time affects what things mean, it needs to be considered an important element in communication. Attempts to improve how we interact should include a careful examination of when things were spoken, reacted to, or neglected. In particular, time driving, which adjusts meaning of behavior in a sequence, can be used to clarify what is meant by the behaviors of two people, so that each better understands the other.

Time Driving, Identity, and Togetherness

Mentally healthy people invariably have an identity that includes well-defined expectations for themselves in the future. They can recognize and express their hopes, dreams, and goals, and they spend time doing things designed to achieve what they want. Lidz (1975) has supported this notion, suggesting that mental illness involves, in part, a loss of capacity to direct the self into the future.

When two people enter the dialogue of marriage, they bring with them an identity in one or another stage of development. Some people are secure in what they are, how they act, and what they want, and they are fairly self-sufficient. Others are less confident in some areas and hope to obtain support from their partners.

When the marriage begins, the beliefs, values, and perceptions that make up one's identity are brought into immediate contact with those of another person. Together the two people embark on learning how to join together in a way that is most useful and happy for both. If both of them are secure in how they have organized and developed themselves, they can see fairly clear boundaries between their self-identities and the entity they form as a married couple. When appropriate, they attribute the cause of events to themselves as individuals rather than to the other person. They progress toward individual self-fulfillment by forming mutually supportive sequences of interaction, ones that help them work together or independently to achieve self-determined outcomes.

In contrast, people who are not secure distinguish less clearly between what is part of the marriage and what is within themselves. Instead of forming sequences of behavior to promote achievement of individual expectations for the future, they form sequences designed to help complete themselves in the present. Ironically, when this happens, the very thing that one person wants from the other (e.g., love, support, trust, encouragement, stability) may be in low supply with the partner also. But, being incomplete, each thinks the other is the key to happiness, that he or she can somehow supply what is wanted. For example, a husband who lacks self-confidence may expect his wife to give him what he does not have, and if she fails to do this he may feel righteously indignant. Thus justified in his mind, he proceeds to play games and to exploit or manipulate her for the purpose of completing and securing his own identity. Unfortunately, in all his effort he has focused attention on his wife's actions, attributing causality of his happiness or unhappiness to her, and as a result he fails to consider what he can do himself to obtain his growth goals. He has lost the sense of being a unique and individual person, treating his own hopes and dreams unimportantly and perhaps even forgetting them.

If used appropriately, time driving can help couples find a good balance between individuality and togetherness. If they have become too enmeshed in each other's actions it can help them perceive their separate identities once again, and restore a positive equilibrium. Time driving has this effect because it involves a present-future time orientation. Emphasis is given to what each will do in sequence with the other at a future time. When a couple examine one of their behavioral programs at time A and reorganize it for future time B, each partner is pushed out of attributing causality to the other by focusing on his or her actions at a future time.

Time Driving and Blaming

The following example of a negative communication program illustrates how destructive some sequences can be.

> Bob and Martha report they are unable to talk about anything difficult. When any disagreement arises, he becomes angry

*and she stops talking. Her avoidance so angers him that he
says harsh, demeaning things, often exploding into a tantrum
of stomping, hitting the wall, and other forms of violence.
Seeing his anger, she tries to calm him down, but failing, she
finally gets angry at him and says demeaning things in return. Then, following the actual conflict, they become distant
from each other. He involves himself in work, she experiences
lethargy, depression, inability to work, psychosomatic head-
aches and backaches, and even suicidal wishes. When away
from her husband during this time, however, she is open, out-
going, and friendly to other people.*

An examination of these two people's backgrounds revealed
that each had been conditioned to certain behaviors by the patterns
that existed in their families. Bob had a very difficult relationship
with his mother, which was characterized by nearly continuous
angry arguments. He recalled that once engaged in one of their
shouting matches, neither he nor his mother seemed able to stop.
When he tried as a child, his mother would not permit him to quit,
ridiculing him if he withdrew. Martha, by contrast, grew up in a
home where conflict was avoided if possible, and things "were
seldom discussed until we cooled off." Once married, both exhibited behavior they had learned as part of a similar context in
their family background.

What should be done in a case like this? The answer is not
to focus on how wrong one or the other may be or on their past
experiences, as many people do. Instead, Bob and Martha need to
work on the sequence that is the real source of difficulty. Blame
for the "problem" need not be placed on either, since both will
need to participate. Through time driving they can concentrate on
identifying their communication program and changing it.

Blaming and accusations are normal human reactions to problem situations. To some degree at least, we usually try to identify
who caused a problem and who is responsible for something bad,
so we can punish the wrongdoer. In courts of law this inclination
is quite appropriate, but in marriage it is not effective because there
is seldom just one who is at fault, one who hurts the other, one

who is the victim, or one who should be accused and found guilty. The lives and actions of both are so intertwined that one person's actions are nearly always justified in his or her mind because of what is done by the partner. Watzlawick et al. (1967) wrote that because of the time element which forces one to act, followed in sequence by the other, and so forth, each person views his or her own actions as something sandwiched between two behaviors of the other. While this makes it easy to assume that the other person causes something, the facts simply are that both share responsibility for nearly everything of consequence between them.

Even if a couple accept responsibility, however, they may not know what to do to change matters. Both people usually have to reorient their thinking. Time driving can help them do this by focusing attention on the timing of their actions rather than on who is to blame for what.

APPLYING THE TECHNIQUE OF TIME DRIVING

Having examined the relevance of time driving to improved marital communication, let us now see more precisely how the technique is put into operation.

Identifying the Marker

Bateson (1972) writes that communicational events (behavioral programs) are triggered by what he calls *context markers*. For example, if dinner guests saw a table set with paper plates, they would tend to exhibit a different set of actions than if the table was decoratively placed with fine china, crystal, and silverware. The difference in behavior resulted from observing a particular marker.

For each situation there may be several different markers. The beginning of sexual activity, for instance, may be marked by open affection, caressing, or even verbal inquiry. Some conversational contexts are marked by the topic. The subject of in-laws may trigger a different set of actions than religion or politics. The first task in time driving, then, is to recognize the cue that marks the onset of a behavioral program between the couple. Instead of trying to discuss the whole problem, both concentrate on finding the specific time something happened, where it happened, the people who were present, and what they were trying to accomplish when together. Instead of thinking, "We don't like being with each other," for example, they identify when they do not like being with each other, and how undesirable events begin. There may very well be more than one context marker, perhaps different for each person.

An authentic experience of a couple can be given to illustrate this principle.

> *Ron and Esther Hansen had been married approximately six years. Both agreed that they argued too much. Not only did the arguing create unhappiness, but nothing they did seemed to help, so both felt pretty hopeless about improving things. They began time driving by asking themselves when the arguing occurred. They identified one situation as the time when Ron returned from work and greeted Esther. Shortly after he walked into the house they frequently, though not always, had an argument. Since there were times when things did not evolve into a conflict, they decided to find out what the difference was between a good greeting and one that led to a conflict. At this point, Ron had some insight. He said that he could not always clearly identify how his wife was feeling. If she had had a good day and was openly pleasant, arguments seldom occurred. But if he could not "read her," he did not know how to react, and this, he believed, was typical of the times when they argued. With some interest Esther noted that when Ron looked as if he had had a good day and was happy, things seemed to be better for her. But when she thought he was not happy and tried to help, this led to conflict.*

At this point, Esther and Ron had identified the context markers that seemed to signal the onset of an argument. The markers were, for Ron, uncertainty about how Esther felt, and for Esther, seeing some signal that Ron had experienced a bad day.

Note what was happening to the Hansens. They were both engaged in an attempt to pinpoint the time when their problem occurred and the marker which triggered an undesirable sequence. Though upset, they recognized that blaming each other was unproductive. Each was implicitly accepting a share of responsibility for the problem and for finding a solution.

Identifying the Sequence

The next step in time driving is to hunt for and find the specific sequence of behavior in the program. Note that it is not enough for a person to merely say, "I was upset," or, "You were really grouchy." While these statements may be true, descriptions that are so general and isolated will not reveal how each person's actions fit into a sequence with the other's.

In our example, after Ron and Esther had identified the markers that led to quarreling, they proceeded to explore their sequence of behaviors.

> *Ron said that if he was unable to clearly discern whether his wife was happy or unhappy he tested her a little. One method of testing her was to give her a mild embrace and a "peck" instead of a kiss. When she was happy she usually asked for and got more. Another method was to ask questions about her day. If she talked openly and smiled it meant she had had a good day, but if she spoke tersely he concluded she was in an unhappy mood. In response, Esther said she interpreted a "peck" from her husband to mean that he may not have had a good day. So if she was "pecked" instead of kissed she tested him by giving him a vigorous response. If he returned her affection warmly, it meant that he had had a good day and all would be pleasant. But if he did not respond to her attempt to be more loving, she concluded that his day had not been good and that she should be prepared for an uncomfortable evening.*

Note that Ron and Esther were specifically picking out how each acted. Ron, when he was uncertain about Esther's feelings, gave her a "peck" as a way of finding out what mood she was in. Esther, mistaking the meaning of his "peck," used a vigorous response as a way of finding out what mood *he* was in.

What happened in the next part of their sequence was even more revealing.

> *When asked what he did when he concluded that his wife had not had a pleasant day, Ron said, "I try to leave her alone because when I am in a bad mood I usually want to be by myself." And Esther replied, "I know you do, but that makes me mad. When I am down I want to be talked to and when you leave me alone, I think you are insensitive and uncaring."*

Thus they uncovered a significant factor in the arguments they wanted to stop. Ron had never understood why Esther always insisted on trying to talk to him when he was down, since at such times he wanted to be left alone. Now he recognized that she wanted to be talked with during her bad moods, and thought she was being helpful if she talked during his. Esther was surprised to learn that her behavior was the opposite of what Ron wanted. Now they both realized the crux of their problem: If either was in a bad mood, the other responded inappropriately to it. This led to the argument and the resulting distance and frustration.

Reorganizing the Sequence

Once a couple have specifically described their sequence in the problem situation, they need to organize a new sequence. This means they need, first, to either create new markers or clarify old ones, and second, to determine what behaviors will constitute a more effective sequence.

> *One reason Ron and Esther had difficulty, for example, was the ambiguous nature of the markers. Uncertainty about each other's feelings usually led to an argument. To avoid this Ron and Esther decided to begin by doing something that would clearly evidence their end-of-day feelings. Ron suggested that on his bad days he would drop his briefcase in the foyer so*

his wife would clearly hear it. Esther decided that on her bad days she would wear an apron backwards. When neither had a bad day, which most frequently happened, then they could do anything they pleased. When Ron signaled his "glunks" Esther was to respond by keeping herself and the children away from him for 45 minutes so he could be alone. Following this time he agreed to join the family, but she was not permitted to ask questions unless he indicated he wanted to talk. Then she could inquire about what was wrong and see if she could help. When Esther signaled her bad day, Ron agreed to respond by going to her immediately and talking with her. She believed this would help her get over her feelings faster. In addition, Ron agreed to help her with dinner or housework, rather than reading the paper or doing something else.

Let us summarize what has happened to this point. First Ron and Esther identified the old markers and the behaviors that occurred in a bad sequence. Then they selected new markers, one for the wife and one for the husband. Finally, they planned two new sequences, each tied to one of the markers.

Evaluating Time Driving

After there has been time to practice a new sequence of who will do what and when, it is important to evaluate the effectiveness of the time driving procedure. This, like organizing a new sequence, can be planned in advance. Its purpose, of course, is to help the new behavioral program work as planned and to readjust it if necessary.

Ron and Esther set a time at which they would meet with the counselor and evaluate what had happened. As far as the markers were concerned, both reported them helpful but said they hoped they would eventually sense each other's feelings without having to rely on the briefcase or the apron. The chances for this were quite good, since the physical cues, being paired with the feelings of each person, would help both people to more accurately recognize the feelings from other signs. As for their performance of the new sequences, in general this had gone well. However, one night they encountered something neither had planned. Ron came home after having a particularly bad day. He dropped his briefcase in the foyer as his signal and was on his way to his den for 45 minutes of seclusion when he found Esther with her apron on backwards. For a moment, they said, there was a certain strain and tension in the air.

They thus planned a new sequence for that event. In summary, during evaluation both reviewed what each had done and when. The conversation examined the specific words and actions as they occurred in sequence with each other. Most of the time, the couple decided, their markers and the subsequent interchanges were effective.

TIME DRIVING: SUMMARY AND CONCLUSION

To clarify the process of time driving we shall now summarize what has been said so far. At the outset, it is necessary to identify a situation that needs to be changed, or possibly a future situation in which a couple anticipate that trouble may arise. Care must be taken to focus on only a single context—a specific time that something happens, the people present, their purpose or goal, and where the event takes place. The couple can then get into the process itself, which consists of four steps. These are outlined as follows:

Step 1.   Identify the marker that signals the beginning of an undesirable sequence.

Step 2.   Describe how each person acts toward the other in sequence. Learn what each part of the sequence means to each person.

Step 3.   Organize a new sequence, including new markers and a new series of sequential acts involving both people.

Step 4. Set a time for evaluation; at that time review whether the plans made actually worked as desired, and readjust the sequence of behavior if needed.

Results of Time Driving

The most obvious result of successful time driving is improved handling of a specific marital situation. But there are other results, less apparent, that warrant mention. One of these is a mutual feeling of being in better control of events. When events seem to repeat themselves in unconstructive patterns, it is common for us to feel out of control. Time driving gives us a mechanism by which to manage what happens to us, and it typically brings feelings of confidence in our ability to improve a relationship. In effect, it helps us realize that "we have the power to create much of what we experience."

Another result of time driving, actually a further consequence of what has just been said, is the enrichment of the marriage. When we are freed from the worry that a negative sequence lies ahead, we are more ready to organize things so they are fun, or productive, or fulfilling. We can introduce increased varieties of opportunities and experiences, renewing and enhancing our relationship. This positive attitude will be evidence of a marriage satisfactory to both people in it.

CHAPTER 9
MANAGING CONFLICT: HOW TO FIGHT PROPERLY

Marriage creates many opportunities for tension, insecurity, and stress. These emotions may erupt into open conflict, or they may be channeled or suppressed so that conflict is disguised and not fully expressed. Because we think of love as a peaceful phenomenon, marriages experiencing conflict are usually considered unloving. This is unfortunate, for conflict can exist precisely because we both care for each other. Although many people believe that conflict is the cause of divorce, conflict by itself is neither indicative of the lack of love nor evidence that the marriage is failing. Rather, it is the *failure to successfully manage conflict* that results in divorce. The acceptance of some conflict as a reasonable part of living together, when joined with an effective plan for managing conflict, gives us confidence we can weather the challenges of married life.

If a couple mistakenly thinks that the very presence of conflict is evidence of a poor marriage, they may adopt suppressive strategies. They may pretend tension does not exist, saying when asked, "Oh no, nothing is wrong." By mutual agreement, when the anger which they fear makes an appearance, they draw apart from each other, cool off, and reunite later, assuming it has disappeared.

Never openly acknowledging the existence of conflict, they can live for years with disguised anger and masked tension, never resolving the struggle between them.

On the other hand, if a couple think that conflict is inevitable but do nothing to manage it, they are equally bad off. When tension exists, angry sarcastic rebukes come forth. Both partners may engage in the struggle until tired, then retire a distance only to fight again another day. This strategy resolves very little even though parts of the marriage are strewn around, scrutinized, and bickered over. In contrast to both of these approaches, a good plan of conflict management enables a couple to deal successfully with their tense and angry moments. Thus the purpose of this chapter is, first, to describe some sources of conflict and, second, to suggest how a couple may work together to manage conflict constructively.

SOURCES OF MARITAL CONFLICT

It is commonly believed that the causes of marital conflict are money problems, sex, child rearing, in-laws, or any other topic frequently discussed while a couple is angry. In fact, however, they may not be the causes at all. Although improvement in money management or sexual relations, for instance, may reduce the intensity or frequency of quarreling, usually problems in these areas are only pretexts for fighting about things that are more basic and more complex. In effect, the couple often select any convenient topic that will permit them to talk while trying to fulfill another purpose. For example, if a wife feels her husband to be too dominant, she may participate in an argument about money, hoping to win and reduce his control.

Successful management of conflict depends on understanding the true sources of conflict and doing something about them. Most conflict stems from conditions that exist in every marriage simply because people live together. One difference between marriages with high and low conflict is the way these conditions are responded to. Among the most important factors that relate to conflict in marriage are the quantity of information and quality of leadership. Other sources of conflict are value disagreement, discrepancies in role performance, failing to productively achieve goals, the existence of inconsistent rules, and ineffective communication. Let us examine each of these before we consider how a couple can form a problem-solving plan that will help them to adjust to the sources of conflict in their own marriage.

Low Flow of Information

Chief among the conditions for marital conflict is inadequate flow of information between the partners and also between them and their social environment. The restricting of information flow can happen in many ways. Failure to share varieties of ideas, lack of reading or other mental stimulation, refusing to take time for conversation, and limited social contact are frequently evident in conflictual marriages. Information flow is also inhibited by excessive complaining, criticism, pessimism, or continually focusing on only one or two topics; one partner typically becomes unwilling to talk with the other for fear of being criticized and blamed.

Of course, the common pressures of living sometimes reduce the amount of information-sharing that a husband and wife can engage in. Long working hours, for example, may tire a man or woman past the point of wanting to talk. Financial pressures that force attention on necessities for survival may consume time that would otherwise be available for companionable talk. Similarly, spending too much time on internal family problems and not enough time relating to the world outside can create the condition of low information-sharing.

A low flow of information sets the stage for conflict in several different ways. First, when we expect to know things and do not, we usually suspect negative things. Our lack of knowledge provokes anxiety, which leads us to look for the worst. Second, the absence of sufficient information produces fewer behavioral opportunities. That is, when we do not know or practice a variety of ways of acting toward each other, we become caught in situations and react the same way again and again. Third, if we do not communicate freely within the marriage or with a variety of other people, we tend to feel isolated. When tensions mount, there is no available way to release them except through involvement with the partner. And marriages flounder when they are required to handle all of the emotional needs of both people. Fourth, when communication is restricted, we develop fewer friendships. If we relate only to one or two people (e.g., a friend or family member) we tend to take them into our confidence more than is desirable. Repeated conversations with such a friend increase the chances that we will seek emotional support from him or her, especially with regard to marital problems, and then we become resentful that the spouse does not seem to care as much as the friend. When a married person uses another individual in this way, the two often create a coalition against the spouse, pressing marital communication into yet narrower channels. Furthermore, after seeking support from a friend and telling all, we may at first feel better but we then return to the marriage only to find matters unimproved and perhaps worse. The situation parallels that reported by counselors who see only one person in troubled marriages; under such conditions, they say, divorce happens more often than when both are included.

It seems clear that conflict in marriage can be reduced if both people actively work to increase the flow of information between the two of them, have an appropriate amount of communication with other people, and participate together in enjoyable social activities.

Lack of Agreed Leadership

Lack of agreement about the form of leadership in marriage is another source of conflict. Some couples, for instance, never get around to determining who will make certain decisions, how to resolve differences of opinion, and how to consider and incorporate the opinions of each other. Then when choices have to be made, or when differences exist, they fail to respond effectively and become side-tracked into a hassle over who gets to decide or whose opinion is going to be accepted as the "right" one. Eventually, any difference of opinion that arises in normal married life can signal a new round of "Who gets to be the leader?" Old fights are remembered and built upon because the quarrel seems to be about the same thing, and is only enlarged upon as time passes. Meanwhile, the unresolved differences of opinion produce a backlog of problems which only serve as fuel to the fires of conflict in subsequent arguments.

In low-conflict marriages, leadership roles vary and are flexible, but they are definite. Each partner knows most of the time who will make certain decisions, and the couple have found and adopted ways of resolving differences of opinion. This pattern creates confidence that responsible leadership will exist, because any failure or irresponsibility can more accurately be traced to its source.

Marital leadership usually is a combination of past learning and correct application. All too often, however, a man or woman who has learned good leadership skills at work is unable to apply that ability within the marriage. And it is not unusual for a wife or husband to be lacking in leadership skills altogether. Firm opinions are not expressed, little direction is given by either, and neither seems able to follow through, give directions and suggestions, share honest opinions, and gracefully resolve disagreements. All of these are necessary leadership skills, and their absence is a certain source of marital conflict.

Value Conflict

One characteristic of every human being is the existence of beliefs or values which shape what we think is right or wrong, good or bad, acceptable or unacceptable. These values shape the perceptions we have of other people and things, and they influence how we carry out activities and perform our roles as husband and wife. It is reasonable to expect that the values of one person may be somewhat different than those of the other. But, while differences in values can be a source of stimulation and vitality, they can also be a source of problems. This is particularly likely to be true when a person holds to his or her beliefs with great rigidity and dogmatism. Another person may believe the same thing as a dogmatic person but, being more flexible, will concede the possibility that other ideas may be valid as well. Thus both the existence of differences in values and the degree of rigidity can be conflict conditions.

Cleveland and Longaker (1967) suggest there are some general value differences that more frequently spawn anger and frustration in a marriage. One of these, already discussed in Chapter 6, concerns the way an individual prefers to satisfy material needs—whether that person wants to save and plan for long-range gratification or to seek more immediate gratification. Both orientations are represented within our society, and when one spouse holds to the first while the other values the latter, many conflict situations may arise. The attempts of one to delay fulfillment, hoping to realize it later, will appear to be sabotage by the other person, who, wanting things in the present, will feel frustrated by the conservative planfulness of the other.

Another difference in orientation is represented by the value accorded to status and material success, as opposed to satisfaction derived from rewarding interpersonal relationships. Either goal requires an investment of time and effort, and one cannot usually be pursued without sacrificing the other to some extent. If husband and wife disagree about where the emphasis should lie, conflict is likely.

A third difference that may set the stage for conflict is an orientation toward individuality and independence as opposed to doing things together. If one person prefers to do many things alone, spending relatively little time with the spouse, while the other wants to do many things together, conflict may soon erupt. One partner is criticized for not doing his or her own thing, while the other is accused of low involvement in the marriage relationship. Both are trying to live in accordance with their values, but some balance needs to be struck between the two ideas.

These are just a sample of the value differences that can lead to marital conflict. At this point, it is important to stress that the existence of differences is not inself bad. What happens depends less on the degree of difference in what is valued than on the degree of rigidity with which each partner holds to his or her values. Dogmatic and rigid thinkers, feeling threatened by value disagreements, try to eliminate varying viewpoints and typically produce more conflict. But partners who recognize the inevitability of difference usually try to accept in each other what they cannot successfully compromise. In other words, they learn to live with a difference instead of letting it disrupt their marriage.

Discrepancies in Role Performance

In Chapter 7 we discussed the difficulties that can arise in connection with the way a husband and wife perform their perceived roles. If a man's role as male and husband meshes well with the woman's role as female and wife, conflict in this area is minimal. But if the way one person performs his or her role does not allow the other to perform as he or she thinks best, both partners will be adversely affected. Suppose a man has learned that his role is to provide for and protect his wife, but he marries a woman who has learned to be independent, career-oriented, and successful in her work. She does not need his income nor, because of her independence, much of his protection. Wanting to be a success as a male, he will nevertheless try to provide for and protect her. This, however, may very well interfere with her role performance. Unless they find a way to resolve this dilemma, conflict may become severe.

Another type of role discrepancy arrives when some task that is necessary to maintain a happy relationship is omitted from the roles of both partners. Suppose, for instance, that both people require a great deal of support and encouragement, but neither has learned to nurture another and be considerate as part of his or her total role performance. Conflict will typically erupt, because each is vainly looking for the other to perform a function that is important to both.

Sometimes a person's perception of his or her role contains built-in barriers to good communication, as exemplified by the following.

> Carl believed it was important to not talk about his work,
> even though he was required to work late several evenings
> in the week. But his failure to come home at a particular time

led his wife to suspect there might be something going on that she should know about. When she questioned him, however, Carl invariably withdrew. He did this to avoid having to comply with his wife's demand for information, but his avoidance only increased her suspicions. She therefore accelerated her attempts to get her husband to reveal how he spent his time. By the time he finally told her the truth, her suspicions had been so aroused that she did not believe what she heard.

This conflict was the result of inaccurate perception by the wife of the way the husband saw his marital role, and was traceable to his own failure to adequately communicate and define the role he wished to perform.

As we indicated in an earlier discussion, a discrepancy between our self-expectations and our performance can lead to conflict of a different nature. Many of us have quite firm mental images of how we prefer to act. When we perform our roles in the way we think we should, we are likely to feel good about ourselves, but when we do not, an inner conflict develops. One way of easing the discomfort this produces is to blame someone else. A person who habitually accuses someone else of failings may well be signalling his or her own sense of failure to meet self-expectations for the performance of a role.

Low Productivity

Being able to achieve goals and accomplish tasks is a necessary ingredient for a happy marriage, because marital esteem seems to be closely related to how productive a couple can be. When husband or wife do not act to efficiently accomplish tasks, then conflict may easily appear. At first one person may get angry that something has not been done. If the spouse responds by performing the task, the first person will thereafter consider anger an effective means of getting action. But this approach has two drawbacks. First, any performance motivated by the anger of another person tends to be short-lived and erratic. Second, the person who gets angry must make a show of being highly responsible or risk being called a hypocrite. So he or she tends to take on additional tasks, attempting to show how productive he or she is, while the other avoids contact as much as possible, until they do very little together.

Couples with low productivity may try several other strategies besides getting angry at each other. They may attempt trade-offs ("I'll do this if you do that"), and these sometimes work. They may resort to nagging and criticism, but like anger these tend to produce only short-term success. They may ignore the problem and hope it will disappear, but usually performance does not improve. Solving conflict when productivity is low may require help from a professional who can objectively disentangle the snarl of mutual criticism and improve the productivity of both people.

Inconsistent Rules

Haley (1963) has described the kind of conflict that results from disagreement about marital rules, including who sets them, the kind of rules that exist, and what happens when rules are incompatible. A rule, as used by this author, refers to a practice or pattern of behavior. The complex nature of marriage requires the setting of many such rules. To the extent that conflict revolves around who sets the rules, it is similar to that resulting from lack of clear leadership. To the extent that it revolves around the kind of rules, it is similar to conflict over role performance or values. So far, however, we have not discussed the conflict presented by the existence of incompatible rules. This situation arises so often that it warrants separate consideration.

The setting of marital rules is often a haphazard, casual procedure. Neither husband nor wife may remember very well, from one time to the next, what has been said. Thus a person may try to establish one rule at one time and another one at a subsequent time, without realizing that if the first is followed, the second cannot be. Although examples of this situation are numerous, the following case illustrates how it may occur.

The Wrights seemed to agree that either of them could set rules but Tom had the final say. Both said they usually were satisfied with the rules they created in their marriage. Conflict, however, still existed. At one time, when asked what they wanted from each other, each made a list. Tom said he wanted his wife to provide a cleaner home, spend more time with him, lose weight, and be more responsive sexually. She had a list of equally reasonable things. Both reported that Tom seemed to get angry because he failed to get the things he wanted. He was asked if he exploded about all of them at once. "No," he said, "Just one or two at a time, usually." From further probing, however, it became apparent that his wife could not keep as clean a house as he seemed to want and at the same time spend more time with him. Neither could she be more responsive sexually at one time when he was criticizing how she looked (i.e., overweight) at another time. Nothing seemed to change because Tom was trying to set up inconsistent rules.

Self-Contradictory Communication

Sometimes conflict arises simply because the partners are not good at expressing their wants. In this connection, it is useful to recall our earlier discussion of the two levels of communication described by Bateson—the "report" and the "command." The report aspect is the meaning of the words; the command aspect is the tone of voice and other nonverbal cues that tell the hearer how to receive the message. Thus "kidding" or teasing can only be understood as such if accompanied by laughter and smiles, since the words have a derisive meaning. Whenever the meaning of the words and the nonverbal cues contradict each other, the receiver has to choose between two meanings. What happens, for example, if a person complains but after complaining frequently laughs? The laughter seems to contradict or disqualify the report of the complaint. This means that the partner will probably disregard the complaint. One wife seen in counseling was very upset because her husband did not seem to treat her complaints seriously. She became extremely angry because his response was so minimal, yet she was completely unaware that she tended to laugh whenever she complained. Thus a self-contradictory style of communication became an important source of conflict.

CONFLICT AND BEHAVIOR CHANGE

Having identified some sources of conflict, let us return to the point we made at the beginning of this chapter and consider what conflict can mean. If there is none, does it mean the couple are blissfully happy? If two people argue, do they hate each other? If they are to create an effective plan to solve problems, what is the best way to think of conflict?

Probably because of romantic notions about marital bliss and happiness, to many people the presence of anger and conflict seems to mean that love is gone or is being lost. Of course, married people do not feel loving and tender during a fight; but while conflict and lost love may occur together, they do so much less frequently than we think. Most of the time the anger and hostilities of conflict do not relate at all to the loss of love. Love represents the commitment each has for the other and it is broader than the anger occasioned by a given conflict. More often than not, conflict exists because of the emotional investment two people have in each other, not in spite of it.

Not recognizing this truth, couples may conjure up many negative explanations or interpretations of conflict when it arises. One partner may suspect the other of some unfaithful or spiteful act. A wife may view her husband as purposely starting fights so that he doesn't have to become involved with the family. Or a husband may think the wife argues to distract him from sex. In a different vein, some couples may think that expressing anger and having quarrels are ways of stating the "truth" or allowing both to say what they really feel. These couples mistakenly believe that things said in anger are more accurate than what is said calmly. Only infrequently is this the case.

The worry that is occasioned by conflict depends on the intensity and frequency of it. Increased amounts tend to mean that something is seriously wrong, and small amounts that are not too intense are more easily passed over. Conflict that occurs regularly usually gets tied to something else—lack of sleep, for example, or sexual problems, chronic illness, or in-laws. Once tied to a "cause," conflict then becomes routinely expected and is more confidently endured. Every time the external "cause" rears its head, both people think, "If I can just ride this out things will get better." The trouble is that conflict then tends to get built into a relationship, occupying marital space that could be filled with more beneficial things. Thus, while a couple may be less shaken by habitual conflict, they sacrifice much of their potential for experiencing feelings of intimacy and satisfaction.

What all of this suggests is that instead of focusing on who causes problems, how often they occur, or how intense a conflict is, a couple should start thinking in terms of how to manage conflict. They can do this if they change the interpretation they give to conflict when it arises. Rather than see it as evidence of lost love, suppose they view the presence of conflict as a signal that one or both partners need to change their behavior in some way. This matter-of-fact approach helps a couple to focus on what behavior to change and how to do it, rather than on who started the fight or whether the two people still love each other. This will put them on the road to handling their conflict constructively.

CREATING A FOUNDATION
FOR CONFLICT MANAGEMENT

In this section we shall describe some preliminary steps to follow in developing an approach to conflict management. We shall then turn to some specific techniques that couples have found.

Identifying the Conflict Style

In Chapter 2 we discussed the different patterns of interaction that may characterize a relationship. Interaction styles are particularly evident in conflict situations, for, though it may seem that one quarrel is not like any other, there is usually a definite pattern. So far, three general types or patterns have been described in professional literature (Bateson, 1972; Lederer and Jackson, 1968; Watzlawick, Bevin, and Jackson, 1967). Knowing which type they experience can help a couple to develop more appropriate methods of resolving conflict.

In *complementary* interaction, the wife and husband tend to behave in opposite ways: dominant-submissive, talkative-quiet, active-passive. When they find themselves in conflict situations, they typically behave in one or more of the following ways.

★ One person lectures or sermonizes the other, telling what "should" or "should not" be done, while the other sits and listens.

★ One person tends to become increasingly unresponsive as time goes by.

★ One tries to get the other to change in order to make things better.

★ The angrier one gets the more subdued the other becomes.

★ One may experience depression or other symptoms requiring caretaking by the other.

★ One usually talks much more than the other during an argument.

★ Only one interrupts, while the other adopts a retiring or withdrawing manner.

★ After the argument, when one wants to make up the other is angry and resentful, which perpetuates the cycle.

★ Both try to resolve problems by arguing about who is right and who is wrong. Few compromises are reached.

A second style of interaction is characterized by similarity of behavior, and is therefore called *symmetrical*. In this case, both people act almost identically toward each other. In a conflict situation they may say different things to each other, but their tone of voice, the intensity of their anger, and their nonverbal communication are quite similar. Couples of this type may display the following behaviors.

★ Both try to control each other.

★ Both try to get the other to change while ignoring themselves.

★ Partners match each other in intensity of anger, each shouting, using sarcasm, and belittling the other.

★ Problems or weaknesses in each person are regularly brought up.

★ Arguments tend to be about the same "old" things without any apparent solution.

★ Neither partner talks about personal things, thinking it unsafe to do so.

★ A feeling of competitiveness exists, with both trying to "win" or "get the best of the other."

★ Each person seems to "save up" the mistakes the other makes, so that when an attack comes each has some ammunition.

★ Both interrupt and neither listens very well.

In a third interaction style, called *parallel* interaction, the behaviors of two people are neither opposite nor similar, at least not as a function of the interaction itself. Thus when conflict arises, they do not strike sparks off each other, but instead retreat along separate, nonconverging avenues of behavior. Some of the characteristics of parallel conflict are as follows.

★ Frequently both pretend that no real conflict exists.

★ When anger is present, both may avoid talking to each other, going their separate ways to "cool off."

★ Rather than fully discuss a difficult issue or question, both seem to not want to talk about it.

★ One or both tend to think that "peace at any price" is better than arguing to solve problems.

★ Gaps begin to develop in the relationship, neither feels free to talk, and both gradually come to believe they are misunderstood.

★ Both eventually become involved in separate activities, rather than spending time together.

★ Both tend to feel equally responsible for things that go wrong, but changes are not often made by either.

Although we have treated these three styles of conflict as separate, any marriage may contain some parts of all three. Usually, however, one of the three is more prominent. This suggests that it may be fruitful to examine our conflict style before trying specific techniques. Is our behavior automatically opposite, as in the complementary style? Do we react in ways that are too much alike, as in the symmetrical style? Or do we fail to face things directly, hoping the problem will go away, like couples with parallel conflict? Knowing which type exists can help us to apply an appropriate method for managing conflict.

Renouncing the Search for a Cause

Most of our society believes that the best way to solve a problem is to find out what causes it and then eliminate the cause. That form of logic may work for many things, but in marriage it may be harmful. Suppose an argument stimulates a couple to begin searching for its causes. They will typically trace the events that occurred before the fight. No one likes to be at fault, and since the argument was something undesirable, neither husband nor wife likes to think he or she is the cause. But, not knowing what else to do, they continue to try to locate the cause of the argument, and in so doing may easily find themselves once more in the midst of an argument.

One reason it is difficult to trace the cause of an argument is that we tend to be aware of the actions of only one individual at a time, whether these are our own or those of a spouse. We are usually not able to perceive the dynamics of the whole interaction. When we talk about events that happen to us in our marriage, we speak of what "I" did or about how "you" acted. Most often, however, the problem stems from events that happen between people, events that we participate in simultaneously. Lacking the proper language for analyzing this, we usually end up pointing to either individual rather than to the interaction between us.

Instead of hunting for causes as a means of solving problems, then, it is more productive to look for what might be changed in our interaction. What do both of us want? How did both of us act as the argument got under way? Are there ways of making sure this happens less often? What new behavior could each of us try? These questions presuppose mutual responsibility and pave the way for a progressive movement away from conflict.

Identifying the Attempted Solutions

When a marital problem recurs persistently, despite the best efforts of one or both partners to solve it, the trouble may lie as much in the attempted solutions as in the behavior that prompted them. For example, suppose a wife experiences frequent periods of depression, complains often, and is very pessimistic. The husband, to fulfill his role of helper, responds by (a) giving sympathy and compassion when depression occurs, (b) showing consideration in the face of complaints, and (c) being hopeful when the wife is pessimistic. Logically, this is what his wife needs, but surprisingly, her periods of depression do not cease. She still complains and continues to talk pessimistically. Eventually, the husband gets angry because she seems unappreciative of what he tries to do, and now he blames her for being depressed and so forth. What is the real problem? Is it the wife's moods of depression? Is it some underlying condition causing them? Is it the husband's helpfulness and caring? Most people would say the husband is a very loving individual, but in a way the real problem lies in how he acts, even though his behavior is more socially desirable than the wife's. The real problem *is* the attempted solutions of the husband. For some reason the solutions he has attempted only reinforce the wife's actions and thus serve to maintain a situation that should be changed.

In *Change: Problem Formation and Problem Resolution* (Watzlawick et al., 1974) the authors write that any set of related actions (i.e., depression, complaining, pessimism) will continue as part of the life of the actor if the other person (i.e., the husband in this case) responds by doing something that is either opposite or identical. They also state that the solution to many problems lies in learning what has been done to try to solve problems, then changing the attempted solutions. Thus, instead of trying to cheer his wife, which is the opposite of her behavior, the husband might tell her that if she feels depressed it is all right with him. Almost any response would do, just as long as it is neither exactly opposite nor identical to what the wife does.

Inevitably, married individuals see problems in each other and try to solve them. When change does not soon result, however, it is generally a sure sign that attempts to resolve the problem have instead become part of it. This will happen most often when the interaction style is either complementary or symmetrical. What one person does to try and help is often misinterpreted, bringing about more of the same or furthering the difficulty. To break out of this pattern, a couple can start by stating what each feels the problem to be, then listing what they are presently doing to try and solve it. Frequently, the list of attempted solutions will provide a clue to what the real solution should be.

TECHNIQUES FOR MANAGING CONFLICT

Let us suppose that a couple have identified their style of conflict, have stopped puzzling over causes and started thinking in terms of joint behavior change, and have examined what they are presently doing to try and solve problems. Now it will be helpful to look at some specific techniques for managing conflict.

Stopping Techniques

It may seem odd to think that when arguing or fighting, a couple will agree to work on anything together. Both, however, usually want an argument to stop, and getting a harmful quarrel stopped is an important first step. Consequently, both wife and husband need some mechanisms they can use to abate a quarrel. If their techniques are recognizable to both, either can signal the desire to stop.

Self-narration is a fun thing to do in the middle of an argument. It consists of one person describing how he or she *will* act before the action occurs. Let us suppose that a couple are arguing about the budget. There is complementary conflict and in this case the husband is berating the wife about her mistakes. She tries to explain her side in a fairly quiet, even apologetic voice; but she is frequently interrupted and shouted down. If the wife wants to get the argument to stop by using self-narration, she might say the following.

> Wife: *Here I am talking quietly and in a minute I am going to explain what happened and also apologize for the mistakes I made. Then I'm going to quietly see if I can calm you down.*

There is something a bit comical about one person telling another what he or she is going to do in the next few minutes. Let us see how the husband might self-narrate.

> Husband: *I am going to get angry and yell at you because of your mistakes. And, if you try to speak, I'm going to interrupt you because I'm not going to listen to what you say.*

Self-narration is effective when the speaker carefully describes the actions, words, tone of voice, and feelings that will shortly be displayed. The reason the technique works is that few people can tolerate the idea of consciously planning how they will act during their arguments. The fight tends to stop because neither wishes to be justifiably accused of planning the whole affair.

Over-loading is another stopping technique. To overload the argument, one person throws all of the potential criticisms together into one volley. While each of the "problems" may be legitimate, spewing them all out at once brings the partner up short and thus allows both to stop an ongoing conflict. Suppose a couple are experiencing a symmetrical conflict and neither is listening very well, but both are blaming and accusing each other. Ordinarily this pattern of quarreling is marked by a couple starting with one topic, speaking to it for a few exchanges, then shifting to another explosive topic. Instead of allowing this to happen, husband or wife could overload the interaction by rapidly listing all the things they usually argue about. For example:

Wife: *I would be more responsive if you'd pay more attention to me!*

Husband: *How can I pay attention when you ignore me?!*

Wife: *Besides not paying attention, you don't pay the bills, or spend time with the kids. You are not sensitive to me, and you hate my mother. We have never gotten along because you blame me all of the time and criticize me besides.*

Husband: *What?!*

Wife: *Besides all that, I want to stop this quarrel.*

Overloading, like self-narration, does not in itself change things. What it does do is bring things to a halt for a moment so the couple can examine what they are doing.

Quarrels may also be stopped by using a third approach, the *confusion technique*. Here, one person deliberately acts in a manner so discrepant and contradictory that the other's expectations are confounded. In an argument, as in any other communication sequence, husband and wife have learned to expect certain behavior from each other. The confusion technique, by introducing unexpected behavior, allows the quarrel to be stopped. Because human communication occurs at many levels, there are many possibilities for finding discrepancies, and the more discrepant two things are, the better. Let us look at some examples.

★ Using nonverbal behavior that contradicts the words spoken.

Example: Saying "I am really mad" while touching someone very affectionately.

★ Linking two opposite-meaning statements together.

Example: "As far as I'm concerned you can just bug off and I want you to stay here with me."

★ Saying something obviously false and then, when accused, agreeing.

Example: "I have slaved around here all of the time and you don't do anything!"
"You are out of your mind!"
"You are absolutely right."

★ Labeling something in a way that is obviously incorrect.

Example: "I'm not angry, I am just passionate, that's all."

The confusion technique may appear to be a prescription for ineffective communication, and under most circumstances, it would be. But as a technique for stopping a quarrel it can be very useful. It works because in the face of such blatant contradiction, the receiver has no ready response. During the resulting pause, the sender can extend an offer to stop.

Self-narration, overloading, and the confusion technique are not normal forms of "communication." That is, in ordinary conversation they would occur only where humor was intended. In a conflict situation, however, they can be inserted into the flow of angry messages and, precisely because they are different from what is expected, they can stem the tide of the argument.

Techniques for Changing the Interaction Style

Since the way an argument develops depends on a couple's interaction style, they will handle their conflicts more effectively if they can modify their interaction style. The techniques for doing this will vary according to what that interaction style has been.

Complementary Conflict.   A couple accustomed to complementary conflict can start by identifying the dimensions of oppositeness that characterize their interaction. The following is a list of those commonly present in marriages.

> spectator-exhibitionist
> hopeful-pessimistic
> complaining-cheerful
> clean-sloppy
> dominant-submissive
> close-distant

Note that one person is not, for example, always the hopeful one while the other always the cheerful one. Roles may be reversed from one episode to the next. But whenever one behaves a certain way, the other reacts with nearly opposite behavior.

Let's suppose now that a couple have identified several dimensions of oppositeness but have, quite correctly, chosen to work on just one of these at the beginning. The one they have selected is dominant-submissive. This means that the more dominant one person is, the more submissive the other becomes, to the frustration of both. What can be done? One technique that can be used is called *redefining*. Instead of describing the partner's actions in the same old way, a person describes that behavior in a new way. For example, suppose the (dominant) husband is lecturing his wife, saying (a) she should be careful about driving alone, (b) the roads are dangerous, and (c) something might happen to her if she travels at this time. Previously she acquiesced to his behavior, verbally disagreeing with him but actually submitting. Later she would "zing" her husband, claiming that he was uncaring, restrictive, and the cause of her problems. To redefine she could instead say, "I am glad you are so concerned and interested in me. It is nice to know you care." If said in a nonsarcastic way, the wife's comment will redefine the husband's message, changing it from one of officious supervision to one of caring. Although one might expect this to reinforce his behavior, the odd fact is that he will instead tend to stop lecturing, because this behavior has lost its usefulness as a vehicle for dominance.

In a related vein, one person can legitimize or give tacit *permission* for the other's actions. Thus the wife may say, "You probably have good reasons for what you are saying, so I want you to continue." If the husband is being dominant and continues to be so after the wife gives permission, eventually he has to face the question, "Am I doing this because I want to or because of her request?" His behavior may change in order to avoid letting the wife control things.

Complementary conflict may also be tempered if both people engage in a process called *stating what you see*. Rather than getting caught in the regular struggle, both can, at frequent intervals, state what they observe the two of them doing. One may say, "I notice that when you get more dominant I get more submissive." In a typical complementary quarrel the response to this statement is likely to be disagreement. But then this disagreement can be pointed out as well. When it becomes clear that the focus is on the nature of the actions rather than on what each says, both tend to become more subdued. Both individuals, however, need to apply this technique at the same time to make it work.

Probably the most unusual of all the techniques designed to handle complementary conflict is suggested by Watzlawick et al. (1967). This is to *introduce similarity*. Partners sometimes persist in a complementary style of conflict simply because they think that oppositeness is a hallmark of their relationship. They tend to shrug their shoulders and say, "We're just two very different people, that's all." But usually, as Lederer and Jackson (1968) point out, there are more similarities than differences between marriage partners. By identifying their similarities—whether in mannerisms, beliefs, or emotional reactions—they may perceive each other as being more alike than different. Another way to foster a sense of similarity is to bargain for things. If each can identify one thing that he or she wants from the other, they can develop a trade-off. Not only does each receive something desired, but both are being treated similarly as equals.

A particularly intriguing way of introducing similarity is for each to deliberately encourage some behavior by the other that he or she would normally criticize. That is, each tries to "cause" the other to do what is not wanted, while the other resists the tendency to react as expected. One couple kept a frequency check on two bits of behavior. The husband did not like the wife's habit of disagreeing all of the time and she disliked his tardiness. He tried to get her to disagree and she attempted to get him to be tardy. Each kept a daily chart. The "winner" was to receive a prize of deciding something both would do together. At first both treated the exercise as fairly unimportant. But as one started to keep closer score, the other was forced into competition. By breaking up their habitual reaction patterns they became more nearly similar in behavior.

Finally, couples must recognize that complementary conflict is difficult to change, and may persist despite their best efforts. Because it tends to crop up over and over again, it may require professional help. Doing whatever is necessary is worth the effort, however, since the couple will otherwise continue to experience repeated episodes of pain and frustration.

Symmetrical Conflict.   The management techniques for symmetrical conflict differ somewhat from those applicable in complementary situations. One technique is to *avoid interrupting*. During the heat of a quarrel there is a tendency to act as though "victory" will go to the one who gets more chances to talk. Hence the constant mutual interruptions that are typical of symmetrical conflict. Couples are usually dubious of the value of the no-interruption technique. "Yes, but what if I stop interrupting and my spouse doesn't?" they ask. And at first it may indeed appear that if one partner stops this leaves the other a clear field for "winning." Remember, however, that we are now speaking of a symmetrical style of interaction, and the objective is to modify the conflict pattern. If one partner continues to interrupt while the other does not, they have become more complementary, which is desirable. More often, though, if one stops and announces it, the other feels forced to do likewise, to preserve the similarity that characterizes their relationship. Similarity has not been modified, but now the two people are trying to listen instead of cutting each other off, and this kind of similarity is certainly desirable.

In the same light, it is useful to increase the frequency of *clarification* statements. Stopping to say, "Let me see if I understand you," or any other similar statement, can change the results of symmetrical conflict. Of course, as many married people report, when the chips are down they don't want to try to understand. Instead, they wish to become as powerful as possible as rapidly as possible, and therefore they would rather counterattack than clarify. But stopping any conflict requires some conscious choice to do so. Each person has to decide whether to give vent to feelings and continue the quarrel or do something else that is more constructive. Clarifying is one constructive option.

Symmetrical conflict is marked by communication focusing away from the speaker. Husbands or wives in this style of conflict usually talk about the other person, other things, and past or future events, rather than disclosing feelings or ideas experienced by themselves. Of course, it is difficult to disclose personal feelings in the threatening atmosphere of a quarrel. But some couples habitually keep a lid on their feelings. Then, when each talks only about the other during a quarrel, it is almost always received as "blaming." Thus a cycle of blaming, defensiveness, and counterattacking can emerge because of the couple's failure to self-disclose at other times. Reporting about oneself is always risky, but when the stage is properly set, sharing personal feelings and ideas—possibly but not necessarily during an argument—can help reduce the negative effects of conflict.

Just as it helps to introduce similarity into a complementary interaction, it helps to introduce difference into a symmetrical one. In other words, a couple can deliberately foster dissimilarity in areas where a competitive type of similarity exists. The first step in doing this is to identify some topics that have been the subject of quarrels—sex, money, in-laws, or child-rearing practices, for example. The couple can then create roles for each person that emphasize being different. For example, instead of trying to do everything alike in regards to money, a couple could decide that hereafter one partner will take exclusive charge of paying the bills and organizing the budget, while the other will be solely responsible for something else in the marriage. Regardless of what is selected, the task is to separate the behavior of the two individuals so that differences between them are more often emphasized. The arrangement need not be permanently fixed; at stated times the roles may be shifted from husband to wife and wife to husband. But it should be kept in mind that the purpose is to create differentness.

Parallel Conflict. This type of conflict emerges when married people habitually run on separate tracks, without sharing feelings or ideas, particularly those that seem to hold any potential for direct conflict. But resentments grow and suspicion thrives in an environment that disallows discussion of negative or angry things. Thus, although there may be many good things in the marriage, failure to work through and attend to minor disharmony can widen gaps rather than eliminating them. So the task for couples in parallel conflict is to find ways of successfully becoming involved in resolving differences.

One important thing that can be done is to *metacommunicate*. If a couple start to talk about how they communicate, as recommended in Chapter 8, sooner or later at least one person will comment on the fact that neither of them talks about difficult things or expresses dissatisfaction openly. Recognizing that this is an undesirable state of affairs is an important first step. It is surprising how many problems a couple can avoid discussing, and continuing to not talk will only aggravate parallel conflict.

Having become aware that they need to be more open about their wants, each person should then select one aspect of the partner's behavior that he or she does not like, and propose a goal for change. In the beginning, it may be easier for both to deal with problem areas if a specific program is set up for each person, including rewards from the spouse for specific acts. To help improve one husband's cleanliness around the home, for example, his wife agreed to cook special foods whenever he kept all of his clothes correctly put away. In turn, he agreed to take her to dinner whenever she completed seven days without making snide remarks about his relatives. Eventually, each was able to register complaints and respond to those of the partner without structuring the situation in this way.

Since couples with a parallel pattern attempt to avoid nearly all hostilities, they may benefit by setting appointments to talk out their problems. Back and Wyden (1968) suggest that fighting by appointment has several advantages. Both people have time to think before they get to the meetings, so all of those things they wish to say can be made clear at the right time—not in private post mortems. Furthermore, words tend to be less colored by emotion and more by reason if a brief delay occurs between the thought and the expression. When setting the appointment, the couple should agree to talk about only one issue or concern at that time. The person asking for the appointment identifies what he or she wants to discuss and both agree not to become distracted from it until it is settled. One issue at a time is enough, and with this restriction constructive discussions are more likely to take place.

When a couple adopt the rule of not talking about something as a means of avoiding conflict, they are likewise hesitant to talk about what each needs to be happy. Ironically, people in parallel interaction tend to be more flexible than those with other interaction styles, and each person is usually more than ready to respond to the needs of the other. But this flexibility is wasted if the needs are not stated. Thus it may be useful to spend several sessions discussing and clarifying what each person needs to be happy.

Modifying the Sources of Conflict

In the early part of this chapter, we described some conditions which set the stage for conflict. Although the techniques we have just discussed are helpful in reducing the severity of conflict, it is also important to consider what may be done to solve these basic problems. For instance, if low information flow exists, then a couple should seek ways of increasing their sharing and social companionship. In the chapters on decision-making, negotiating, metacommunication, and time driving, we have provided other suggestions that may enable a couple to deal with their basic sources of conflict.

Finally, it would not be fitting to discuss conflict management without mentioning the obvious need for positive attention to each other in a marriage. Courtesy, politeness, sharing, doing things for each other, enjoying each other's companionship, expressing happiness and love are like preventive medicine. Discriminating between petty and important issues, choosing words carefully, placing trust in each other's intentions, and accepting joint responsibility for everything that happens are all both necessary and wise. Most of all, it is essential that a couple learn to make the most of the time they can spend with each other.

WHO CAUSES IMPROVEMENT

As Julian Rotter (1966) wrote, either we believe that we ourselves control things that happen to us, or we believe that fate, chance, or some other external force does. Both attitudes are shaped by our experiences. If we think we control most of what happens to us, we see conflict as something produced by our own behavior, and therefore as something that can be managed. If we think we are always at the mercy of external forces, we see conflict as something outside of our own doing. With this outlook, we are not prepared to manage conflict and there is less chance that we will actually face and solve problems.

Facing what we fear is, in the long run, a safer approach than avoidance. It is apparent that in many cases a problem, weakness, or even some form of wrongdoing does less damage than attempts to hide it from view. To take an example from psychiatry, fear of snakes is not in itself a serious problem, but if an individual acquires several behavioral mechanisms to hide the fear, those actions will be at least neurotic and possibly worse. And getting rid of inappropriate avoidance behaviors, once these are firmly established, is often more difficult than treatment of the fear that was at the root of them. It is much better, then, to directly face what we fear or find difficult and to resolutely work at resolving it. To do so, we must accept the fact that we share in causing things that happen to us. We must recognize that we are not victims of an unmanageable power.

Behavioral scientists have for years been fascinated by the question whether we feel things because of our actions or vice versa. For example, does a person run because he or she is afraid, or does the person experience feelings of fear because he or she is running? The debate is still open, but we do know that in general, our confidence and self-esteem are higher when we act to face problems rather than running from them. Being convinced that we can manage conflict helps to reduce the fear of conflict. If, instead, we fail to confront our behavior, we become more fearful and apprehensive, and hopelessness soon follows.

Many of us glibly recite that marriage is supposed to help us grow. Then, when conflict tells us it is time to change, we resist growth and deflect responsibility away from ourselves. But, by hiding from conflict, we often produce more hurt than would be the case if we sought the most effective means of improving and then worked at doing so.

Of course, since it involves a two-person communication problem, successful management of marital discord requires the participation of both people, who agree on the need to develop a workable approach. There are times when one person, with professional help, can work out strategies for reducing discord that have at least limited success. In general, however, it is neither wise nor fruitful for only one partner to attempt to manage conflict.

When and if both people agree to work on their problems, they have surmounted a major hurdle. Then, by following the preliminary steps we have suggested—identifying their conflict style, shifting focus from causes to ways of changing, and examining the solutions already attempted—they can prepare to explore a variety of techniques for stopping quarrels and for changing their interaction style. Some techniques will work better than others, and the couple may invent a few of their own. Usually, after some genuine effort, a couple who proceed as recommended will find themselves having fewer arguments. This gives them greater confidence that they can manage, and if they also give thoughtful attention to underlying sources of conflict they can eventually learn to solve problems without painful arguments. That, of course, is the goal toward which they are working in their attempts to manage conflict effectively.

CHAPTER
10
WHAT LOVE IS

Some writers today contend that love is irrelevant to satisfaction in marriage and may even detract from it. According to Lederer and Jackson (1968), for example, successful communication and constructive behavioral exchange are the keys to marital happiness. The idea that we should marry for love or that love is required for happy relationships is a mirage existing in people's minds, they say, because the mutual meeting of needs, accurate communication, and the ability of each to adjust to the personality of the other are far more influential in determining whether marriage is happy.

Much research about marital satisfaction supports this viewpoint. Nevertheless, there is something not made evident in Lederer and Jackson's position. Understanding the word symbols we each use is an important basis for the accurate communication which they consider a basis for marital satisfaction. And since love is the word symbol we are accustomed to use in explaining great varieties of marital events, if actual feelings of love are not a determinant of happy marriages, then mutual agreement about what love means is. It is part of the vocabulary we use to label events and express opinions, and therefore it is valid, even vital, to consider love and the events that symbolize love in discussing the marriage dialogue.

"Love and marriage" have been written, sung, and dreamed about to the point that many of us think of them as inseparable. Supposedly people fall in love and, if all goes well, love each other throughout their marriage. Love is most often given as the reason for getting married in the first place, and loss of love is most often given as the reason for dissolving a marriage in the end. Love with its several attributes, in sex, in sharing, in sacrifice, and in romance is the label for the set of emotions two people offer each other when they mutually commit themselves to a lasting relationship. As we have indicated in earlier chapters, however, it is not enough for two people to share the same feelings; they must communicate these to each other. When love is shown in abundance and in a consistently accurate way, husbands and wives are assured of each other. When it is not felt at all, or when it is felt but not shown, assurance gives way to doubt and worry.

We have already touched on the fact that childhood training may limit our capacity to express our feelings. Instead of permitting emotional reactions to register in conscious awareness, we filter them through a screen of what we think is acceptable, or mask the feelings entirely, due to fear of exposure. In the extreme, instead of forthrightly expressing our emotions, we so disguise them with rational trappings that they do not clearly appear at all. We dissociate ourselves from them, and explain all our behavior in terms of logical principles of human conduct. These logical principles are so general that few exceptions or disproofs can be found, and if we couple this procedure with speaking infrequently about anything we feel, we reduce the risk of suffering pain through rejection or ridicule. Setting up our lives to avoid pain, however, also reduces the likelihood that a partner will know and understand us as a unique and special human being. Furthermore, by inhibiting our expression of feelings in general, we lose the ability to express that which we would like to express, our need and desire to give and receive love. Thus, when a person restricts the capacity to feel and to measure the inward experience, he or she at the same time retards the growth of loving companionship.

Recently, I stood in front of my home watching some neighbor children play a game of kickball. Two boys, aged 12 and 8, made up one team while two girls composed the other. The boys were at bat. The 8-year-old lofted a kicked ball high and far enough to easily be a home run. As he grinningly rounded third base the 12-year-old started yelling, "Go back, go back!" When he saw the younger boy continue to run he yelled louder, "Go back, you nincompoop, you idiot, you can't steal home." When the smaller boy reached home base, the larger grabbed him by the collar, turned him roughly around and shoved him back toward third. All his smiles were gone. Things had become too grim. When he arrived at third base the 8-year-old turned and in a muted voice said, "I see." Watching this, I reflected, "If I were 8 and someone 12 was calling me an idiot, I believe I too would say, 'I see.'"

At dinner with my family a few days after this incident, my children came to the table all excited about something, whispering and laughing. Naturally, I wanted to be in on something so good and I asked them to tell me what excited them. It seemed that their elation stemmed from the fact that a very tough kindergarten girl in our neighborhood had beaten up a first grade boy at school. I was about to chalk this account up to the "experience of children" when it occurred to me that other, similar episodes had been recounted in our home. One involved a "fat boy" at school who was laughed at. One involved my own son, who was rejected by other children. In others my own children were doing some of the hurting and ridiculing. These thoughts and the experience at the dinner table seemed to relate to what had happened during the kickball game. "What are we teaching our children?" I thought, "Am I failing as a parent?"

Then I considered who else may have a role in teaching children. The schools, of course, were obvious. I remembered reading a paper titled *Teaching the Young to Love*, by Jack R. Frymer.*

---

* Paper presented at the NEA convention, Las Vegas, Nevada, 1972.

In it he reported a study of school teachers in the United States. They were asked to rank 54 educational concepts in terms of their importance to education. Twelve of the concepts related specifically to children, dealing with their happiness, independence, and self-esteem. The rest related to such factors as textbooks, salary, administrative procedures, and grading practices. More than 3000 teachers participated in the study. The results were surprising for a number of reasons, but the most surprising finding was that not one of the twelve concepts relating to children was ranked at higher than middle place among all the concepts. That is, teachers apparently thought many factors in education were more important than the children they were teaching. This study, when considered beside my own experience, seemed to confirm that in families and at least schools, we may be failing to adequately teach love. If children learn reading, spelling, and writing, and fail to learn love, have we been successful? If they do not learn love while at home or at school, can they be expected to learn it later during marriage?

Feeling and expressing love for others is not instinctive or natural. It is learned in part through being the recipient of love, and unless love is received in regular amounts from cherished people over a long period of time, the capacity to feel and express it may not be learned at all. Fathers can fail to adequately love their sons and daughters. Mothers can miss sharing it with their children as well. Many children without parents hunger for it. When love is absent from anyone's life, fear and insecurity exist in its place. People deprived of love in growing up tend to approach marriage with the hope that here, the traditional place where love exists, they will be given what they have not received elsewhere. But no idea could be more unreasonable. At the beginning both husband and wife must have at least some love to give and must also be open to receiving it.

Let us assume, though, that two people marry having a relatively good capacity to experience emotions. And, of the feelings experienced, one is love. But, to perpetuate and enhance their feelings, they may still need to learn ways of symbolizing love that can be easily identified. Otherwise, one or both parties may mistakenly come to think that love is not present—not because it is not felt, but because it is not recognized. Keeping in mind that expressions of love in marriage may need to differ from those in other relationships, or may even be unique to the two people, a couple need to arrange marital events, or evidence, to help them conclude that love exists. Each needs confidence that it is there.

THE LOGICAL ORDER OF LOVE

The human brain has the capacity to observe the world, describe and code events, and classify them into categories. A label or name is given to each category, which usually consists of several related concepts. But rather than forming categories one at a time, we actually create them in pairs. In one category we place things that are alike in some respect and in the other we place things that are not similar to those in the first. That is, at the same time as we create a category of happy things we simultaneously create a category of things that are not happy. These need not be "sad" or "unhappy," they are merely "not happy."

Although most people within the same culture have similar ways of categorizing their experience, there are nevertheless some marked differences from one individual to another. Two of these differences are highly germane to whether we believe love exists in a marriage. One is related to the richness of the categories themselves. For instance, in the category of "loving" acts, one person may include many things, while another person includes only a few. As the first person looks out into the world he or she may see many different types of events and consider them to be "loving." The other may see exactly the same things but instead of labeling some of them "loving," considers them something else. This is why one spouse can do several "loving" things and not have them interpreted as such by the other.

Another difference between people's classification schemes is the nature of the concepts they place into their categories. That is, one person may group several abstract concepts together while another focuses on more specific things. For example, one individual may think of love as "the Christian agape" (abstract), while another may think, "love is hugging."

Keep in mind that in regard to love, the task of married people is to create events which evidence it. When it is not manifest one or both may begin to be afraid that they do not love each other. Because happy marriages are tied to the belief that love exists, the absence of love logically means that something must be wrong with the marriage.

The most convincing displays of love are not in the words "I love you." Although nice to hear and important by themselves, these words will not communicate love unless the person also shows love in his or her behavior—for example, by being affectionate, remembering birthdays, or laughing at our jokes. Many similar acts fit into this category, and "loving" is the label that distinguishes them from the wide range of acts that do not match our concept of what is loving. "Unloving" acts—e.g., cruelty, physical abuse—are just as logically related as are "loving" acts. But in addition to these possibilities, one more exists. Things in this category may be collectively called "not unloving." The symbols of "not unloving" are distinct from those of either "loving" or "unloving." If a couple do things that fit logically into the category of love and also do unloving things, like hitting, ridiculing, or belittling each other, there is of course a dramatic contradiction that creates doubt about the existence of love. Even behavior that is not unloving becomes difficult to categorize as simply that. The most convincing evidence that love exists is the combination of behavior that symbolizes love with behavior that is not unloving.

INDIVIDUATION

In the process of maturing many of us only partly learn to see our feelings as something separate from what is experienced by anyone else. Whether we are happy, sad, angry, frustrated, loving, hateful, resentful, or revengeful, we may not accept the emotional state as wholly our own. Then marriage brings us together in the most compellingly close association. In such a situation, if we do not believe our feelings are separate from those of anyone else, it is easy to blame a partner for our emotional states. But when we recognize and accept our emotions as our own, we can more clearly distinguish between what is caused by ourselves and by another. The state of being emotionally separate (i.e., attributing causality of feelings to oneself) is the state of being individuated.

The reason why individuation is a foundation for love may not be readily apparent. But it is a condition that makes it possible to recognize certain acts as not unloving. Each person, realizing that his or her opinions, feelings, and actions are self-motivated, and not caused by the partner, allows for a similar kind of self-selection in the other. Consider the wife who reported the following experience.

> I'd had a bad day. Nothing had gone right and I was pretty frustrated. When we went out later for the evening my husband was happy and joked around. I can't remember for sure what he did but it triggered the feelings I had carried around all day. I really got mad. I was so upset I wanted to get out of the car. To my surprise he got mad too and we just yelled at each other. Later I asked him why he couldn't let me have my feelings and not let my anger affect him.

This wife was making a request difficult to comply with. She herself recognized that her husband's feelings were separate from hers, but he did not. What she wanted was the right and opportunity to express herself without becoming entangled in her husband's feelings. When couples are able to recognize that each person's feelings are separate and most often self-caused, then when something goes wrong, instead of blaming each other the partners each communicate "not unloving" by accepting responsibility for their own emotions. And if one partner says, "I love you," the message is then very clear that "I have a feeling, separate from you, and it is loving." In the absence of unloving acts, this message has accurate meaning. Expressions that are logically related to love appear to be more authentic because they are unfettered by suspicion or malice. Since one person does not control the feelings of the other, then if the couple stay together it must be because love and desire are present.

COMMITMENT AND PRIORITY

Very often love is symbolized by evidence of commitment. Husbands and wives look for signs indicating the level of importance each gives to the other. One indicator of active commitment is the amount of time two people spend together, compared with the time they spend absorbed with other things or people. To some extent, we feel that love is reflected by our willingness to plan and share important events. By the same token, we feel doubt if a partner frequently avoids being with us by scheduling individual activities that interfere, or neglects to take advantage of opportunities to share time with us.

Of course, commitment is also shown by our willingness to do things for our partners. Thus we may work long hours in an office, factory, or home in the name of love. But this method of showing commitment will not convey a feeling of love unless time is also spent sharing the feelings, ideas, impulses, desires, hopes, and dreams that make us human beings. In fact, love may even be obscured from view if all available time is spent, say, working to pay for a comfortable home and nice car. This is why people value physical displays of affection, pleasant conversations where each is listened to, compliments and encouragement. All of these focus attention on the person and not on some task to be performed.

Most successful married people develop ways to show commitment by acting to show the value of each to the other. One of the best examples of valuing is found in a story called *Johnny Lingo*, by Patricia McCreer; we summarize the story below.

Johnny Lingo was a handsome, eligible bachelor living and trading on a tropical island. Many women of his village hoped he would choose them as his wife. As was the custom,

when a man sought a wife he bartered for her. Most girls
were purchased for the price of one, two, maybe even three
cows. Gradually the status, even the quality of a wife come
to be measured by the number of cows her husband paid
for her. If a woman was a three or four cow wife she was
highly favored and as a result held high status in the village
community.

In a hut on the outskirts of the village lived a poor man
named Mokey and his daughter Mahona. His poverty had
embittered him and he was a critical, pessimistic man. Much
of his frustration was taken out on this daughter. "Come
here, you ugly," he would say. "Why couldn't I have a
beautiful daughter so I can be rich?" So critical had he been
of her that it was widely believed that she was not only
ugly, but lazy and worthless as well. Besides, she was back-
ward and shy. With hair in her downcast face few people
even knew what she looked like. Everyone wondered if she
would ever marry. No man in his right mind would pay even
a cow that gave sour milk for her.

One day, Johnny arrived in the village and announced he had
come for a wife. To people's surprise he wanted to bargain
for Mahona, his childhood sweetheart. This news traveled
fast and as Mokey reflected on this positive turn of events
he remembered Johnny's wealth and determined to strike a
hard bargain. As two mats were laid on the ground the
people of the village gathered around buzzing with excitement. They were thinking Mahona would sell for less than
any woman in the history of the village. The two men sat
facing each other. Johnny announced, "I have come to seek
Mahona. What do you ask for her?" Struggling to keep his
courage, the father said, "I will give Mahona for three cows."
His attempt to ask for the high price of three cows and then
settle eventually for a compromise of two was greeted by
the hilarious laughter of the villagers. Some one or two cow
wives were even offended and said as much, thinking that
Mahona was ugly and lazy while they were productive and

desired. Johnny sat quietly until the laughter died. Then in a steady and firm voice he said, "I will give eight cows." Stunned into silence, Mokey could only nod his agreement. Johnny promised to bring the cows in the morning and asked to have the marriage celebration later that same evening.

Shocked, the townspeople drifted to their homes, failing to see Mahona, who had witnessed the proceedings from the nearby forest. "Eight cows," exclaimed Mokey, "I am a rich man!! Johnny Lingo must be crazy." On his way to his home Johnny stopped at the trader's and ordered a lovely mirror in exchange for a rare and valuable sea shell. The trader, having heard of the eight cow purchase, thought vanity to be the reason Johnny paid so much. "He is so self-centered," he thought, "he wants the status of having paid more than any other man."

As the night passed into morning and day, Mokey had decided it was all a joke and the cows would not be delivered. Grumbling and complaining, he berated Mahona with a new humiliation, suggesting she would now be the laughing stock of the entire village because Johnny Lingo would surely not complete the bargain. Pausing in his abuse, he heard in the distance, the sounds of cows and voices. Into view came one, two, three, then finally eight cows. Johnny walked to the hut, held out his hand and said quietly, "Mahona, come with me." Unbelievingly she took his hand and walked self-consciously with him to the marriage feast. Shortly after the celebration began, Johnny sensed her discomfort. While others ate and danced they quietly slipped away into the shadows of the evening.

Almost a month passed until the fine gild-edged mirror arrived. Having heard that Johnny and Mahona had returned from their honeymoon trip, the trader determined to deliver the mirror. Arriving at their home, he found a happy and appreciative Johnny, who seeing the mirror wished Mahona to receive it. As she parted the curtain separating the two rooms, the trader saw a slender, confident and beautiful girl. Taken back, he asked incredulously, "How did this happen?" Johnny answered, "I have loved Mahona since she was a child. I saw how the names she was called made her feel and act ugly. I paid eight cows for her so that she and all who know her would remember that she is an eight cow wife. I knew what she was like, but she had to discover for herself."

Like the people in the community where Johnny Lingo lived, we have our own ways to show that we value our mates. Some of us, like them, bestow on our partners the symbols of wealth or status, thinking that position, power, and money are the best indicators of value. Others choose to show appreciation by praising a mate to others, by consulting his or her preferences before making plans, by foregoing other pursuits to enjoy the spouse's company. Since marriage is a relationship in which commitment is invariably expected, if these or other marks of valuing are not evident, our behavior seems unloving and our marriage suffers.

RECIPROCAL GIVING AND RECEIVING

Almost everyone believes that to love also means to give. So embedded is this thinking that in our more selfish moments we may evaluate the extent we are given to as the means of learning how much we are loved. Unfortunately, we tend to focus on the acts of giving and not on the mutual giving and receiving that is a more accurate symbol. We can offer support, do helpful things, make sacrifices, and share all we have; but unless these acts are reciprocated, giving does not represent love. At least not in marriage. If we wish to help both of us know we are in love, we must give and receive in reciprocity.

There are several reasons why couples may not have a balance in their giving and receiving. Some people do not know what or how to give to the other person. Usually, however, reciprocity fails because we do not know how to receive well. Paradoxically, those who have been deprived of love and so hunger for it the most are the ones least able to receive it. They may offer to give, either out of a sense of duty or from a desire to get in return; but when given to, they distrust the giving as ungenuine. Or they may try to be self-sufficient, pretending to need nothing, in order not to appear dependent or weak. Because they do not know how to receive, they do not form adequate reciprocal bonds.

If one partner tries to be the giver always, and cannot also be a receiver, then love is lost to the view of both. Historically, we have emphasized the giving of love, and we have not given much importance to letting each other know we receive and accept. Yet when one person acknowledges the surety of the other's love, the giver is profoundly affirmed as an accepted and valuable companion. It is here that success in symbolizing love is lost or achieved.

One manifestation that giving and receiving are reciprocal is found in the freedom each feels to grow. In many troubled, so called "nonloving" marriages, one or both partners restrict their own personal growth efforts because they are so caught up in mutual criticism that they don't dare take the time to innovate or create. One wife criticized her husband for "sloppiness" but found herself having to spend several hours keeping her home immaculate so that she could legitimately blame him and not be hypocritical in doing it. In order to maintain this routine and others similar to it, she had eliminated a number of things from her life that would help her grow. Her behavior showed quite clearly that she was not receiving his love. Another couple, at the same time as they complained that each did not love the other, severely restricted their pursuit of individual interests. "He doesn't do things enjoyable for him, so I can't pursue my interests either," was the wife's comment. He had a similar view of her, and so both left much out of their lives.

Identifying activities or experiences that bring growth and participating in them shows both partners that love exists. Within an intimate relationship the personal development and new learning experienced by one partner is viewed, in part, as benefiting the other. The effort a wife makes to be a more stimulating conversationalist, for example, and to be more attractive to her husband, is not only showing love, it acknowledges his. A husband who learns something new and shares it with his wife is acknowledging hers. The increased confidence and esteem resulting from new learning is evidence of what one person's love enables another to do or become. Becoming more confident, risking new things, and exhibiting enthusiasm tell a partner that his or her attempts to give love are being successful.

Another way of acknowledging that love is received is related to the expression of anger. For many of us, anger—from ourselves or directed toward us—is accompanied by a fear of not being loved. By constructively handling anger that is directed toward us we can communicate that we are not afraid that we are unloved. For example, suppose a husband gets angry at his wife; by controlling her own anger and responding constructively, she can assure him that she is confident of his love. There is no need for her to get as angry as he is if she is assured that love is present. As it happens, we often show anger and quarrel at the very time when one or both of us may be insecure about being loved. Since mutual anger makes us afraid we are not loved, fewer arguments would occur and more love would be received if we refrained from responding in kind to another's anger. By refusing to answer anger with anger, we reduce the fear of lost love and gain much confidence in the relationship. In this connection, withdrawal is not the proper way of avoiding anger, because withdrawal implies rejection and may seem but a different form of anger. Helpful responses are to ask for the reasons behind the anger, to seek clarification, to ask whether we can talk calmly, or to suggest that "we can work this out together."

Another way of acknowledging love, as part of reciprocal giving and receiving, is to tell a partner about our hopes and desires for the future. When one person authentically tells what he or she wants to become or to do, it communicates confidence in the other person's caring. Conversely, since we hide our hopes from the view of anyone who we are not sure loves and cares for us, concealment of our expectations for ourselves can communicate a lack of confidence in the partner's love.

One couple had experienced much conflict and distress for the three years of their marriage, and neither partner believed in the other's caring. Much of the conflict centered around the type of work the husband engaged in and whether the wife also should work. They argued about the amount of time he was away from home, how much money he earned, what would happen if she earned more than he did, and many other related issues. When the wife was asked, "What do you really want for yourself?" she said, "I don't know." But then she proceeded to try out a few "ifs" saying, "Well, maybe I would like to . . ." As the conversation proceeded it became clearer that both partners had submerged their own wants in the tide of blaming and arguing. Neither had expressed what he or she honestly wanted, and so neither had communicated confidence in the other's love. When this information was finally shared, they began to believe they were capable of finding solutions.

In summary, although most of us believe that showing love is an important ingredient of a successful marriage, fewer of us realize how important it is for each partner to communicate that he or she knows of the love of the other person. Those who have found much happiness together have learned that pursuit of personal growth, a calm confidence in the other's love, and sharing hopes and dreams for the future help create this important sense of reciprocal giving and receiving.

BENEVOLENT BLINDNESS AND SACRIFICE

Some communication "experts" suggest that an all-pervading openness is the basic ingredient of solid marital communication. It is true that many marriages break on the rocks of failure to communicate at all; it is not true, however, that marriage partners must express directly and pointedly every last shred of their thoughts and feelings, especially where mistakes and shortcomings are concerned. Much harm can result if the creed of honesty and openness is used to justify the act of exposing faults and errors. In fact, it often happens that the behavior to which the most attention is paid is the behavior that is perpetuated. Being open and honest at the wrong time may serve therefore to strengthen the very behavior one wishes would change. Furthermore, openness is useful only if it is applied to things that people can change. It is not useful, and may be hurtful, to criticize a partner for things that are beyond his or her control.

We propose instead that partners adopt a principle of benevolent blindness. This means that though shortcomings may be observed, they are not pointed out unless they are seriously disturbing to the marriage. Opportunities to point them out are sacrificed in favor of noticing positive things. Oddly enough, many a human failing withers and disappears if neglected. This does not mean that hurtful, malicious, or incompetent behavior should be ignored. But many of our faults are of little consequence, and they are best left alone. The effect of not doing so is illustrated in an example reported by a young married woman:

> *At first we were very happy. I remember walking across our college campus and feeling my heart pound when I thought I would see him. The first year of marriage was wonderful. Our sex life was passionate and we did about everything together. I enjoyed being the housewife and doing things for him. I hoped it would go on forever. After we had been married a while, a friend asked, "How can you stand the way he eats?" Until then I hadn't noticed that Don ate noisily. After seeing this I can remember wondering what else my rose-colored romantic glasses had blinded from view. I began to notice how he walked, slept, worked, and played. I began to see things I didn't know were there. This went on until I found myself watching everything he did and it wasn't until later I realized I didn't feel close to him. Our sex life deteriorated and I didn't have that romantic feeling any longer. Now, I almost hate the thought of having to stay married.*

This wife also wondered what would have happened had she not started to look for failings in her husband. There is some chance that the passion might still exist.

Benevolent blindness, as we have described it, is a symbol of love. Suppose a woman knows she has an unattractive mouth or nose, or sometimes does foolish things. If she realizes that her husband is aware of her looks or the way she acts, but does not make a big thing about them, what can she conclude? Most often, she will recognize that she is loved, because her husband acts as if he does not see the defects. All of us are probably more aware of our limitations than anyone else. We are prepared to be criticized for them, even chided or mildly ridiculed. When what we expect does not happen, though it could, we usually consider ourselves loved.

Of course, there are times when we each notice the other observing us and would like to know what he or she sees. But in general, if a problem or an inadequacy is beyond someone's control, it is wise to avoid bringing it under scrutiny. It is best to build on what is good about us both, and not foster disappointment by bringing to the surface an annoyance the other can do nothing to change. And yet, too many of us refuse to let something of this nature alone, but instead bring it up again and again when we would do better to forget it.

This capacity and compassion to ignore is a form of loving sacrifice. By practicing selective blindness we give up something at present for something better in the future. Of course, there is no guarantee we'll get anything at all. There is no foreseeable reward for refraining from criticizing someone else's faults. We are not given a gold star or a lollipop for resisting the temptation to use a defect to hurt or punish. But it is clearly and truly a pure love that motivates this sacrifice of a small gratification for the sake of a better marriage.

THE RITUALS OF RESPECT

Most married people observe rituals that symbolize their love for each other. Some are elaborate, others are quite simple, and their value lies in the meaning given to them by the couple. Many of the rituals we create are associated with special family events like birthdays, days of recognition, or holidays. At these times it is expected that we will expend effort to present gifts and do special things for each other. Doing so provides some recognition of each other's feelings. There are, however, other kinds of rituals that clearly symbolize love. These, the rituals of respect, have great impact because they are derived from the most basic parts of our personalities.

One ritual is that of *protectiveness*. The sorting and sifting of married life reveals vulnerabilities within us all. When we have the courage to disclose them to the view of a loved one, it affords an opportunity for him or her to display protectiveness. For example, a wife, knowing that her husband feels great embarrassment when speaking to others, may exert herself to do more talking and explaining when they are in public. Or a husband, seeing the hurt his wife suffers because their son has committed a crime, may respond by showing increased care and tenderness for her. In some marriages, by contrast, both the husband and the wife feel vulnerable, but they are afraid to reveal their weaknesses. Ironically, the desire for self-preservation deprives them both of opportunities to communicate love, and so in the long run they only wound themselves. Such a situation would not occur if they talked about and understood the areas of potential hurt, and responded with protecting behavior when it was appropriate.

Another ritual of respect is the exercise of *politeness and courtesy*, genuinely extended. Of course, we can go through the mechanics of polite behavior without loving someone. But assuming that love exists, acting courteously toward each other is an easy way to show it. This ritual has many variations. They range from saying, "Thank you," "Excuse me," "I'm sorry," or "Please," to courtesy shown by a husband to a wife, or a wife to a husband, at dinner or the theater. Living together as they do, a couple do not need to observe these niceties. But the small gestures involved can symbolize love all the more because they occur precisely when they need not.

The movement toward sexual equality has prompted some people to proclaim that the conventions of courtesy are no longer needed, and that they are in fact devices which subordinate one person to the other. If only one person shows courtesy this may be the case, but if both do so, then instead of degrading either person it uplifts them both. It is interesting to speculate whether there is any correlation between the deemphasis on courtesy and the increasing numbers of people who fail at marriage. In any case, it is not difficult to speak respectfully to others, to rise when someone enters a room, to offer a seat to one who is tired, to carry a parcel for someone, to stand until others are seated, or to consider another's sense of propriety and stay within appropriate limits. The risks we take in not ritualizing this type of respect are considerable. Instead of upholding the importance of marriage we appear to treat it lightly. Instead of ennobling ourselves with this symbolic display of value, we allow ourselves to seem unimportant to one another. The small effort it takes to practice the rituals of courtesy is therefore well worth while.

INTERNAL CONSISTENCY

In this age of "doing your own thing," many people place a high value on doing the unconventional. Thus we are praised for our flexibility when we create some novel alternative to established expectations. It is also true, however, that we have individual self-expectations and a certain sense of stability or instability in regard to them. That is, all of us are more or less able to identify what behavior we want to display, and all of us, consistently or inconsistently, try to act within self-imposed limits. It is likely that we are happiest when we achieve a good balance between self-prediction and flexibility.

As we learn the interpersonal skills of talking, listening, and expressing emotions and attitudes about people, we formulate a set of criteria suggesting how each of us prefers to act. For instance, one husband might think it unacceptable to hit his wife, but another might have no compunctions about hitting his wife when angry. While we are formulating what is acceptable and unacceptable to us, we also form an idea of what is beneficial to other people. Putting these two together, each person has an internal guide to what promotes his or her own growth and simultaneously enhances the other person. In marriage, it is necessary to exercise self-restraint on both accounts. In our example above, even if a husband does not violate any personal criteria by hitting his wife, he is surely acting contrary to her best interests and is therefore doing harm to the relationship.

The limits of self-restraint are in various states of firmness at the time we marry. To the extent that we are able to act stably within them, we believe ourselves to be successful marital partners. When our behavior is unstable and out of control, we see ourselves as failing and doing damage to ourselves and to the person we married. Restraint, or consistently acting within our self-imposed standards, is a remarkable symbol of love. It is not available to those who may lack the ability to act stably within some prescribed definition. Instability and lack of restraint are thus the opposite of love, symbols of despair and alienation.

Why is self-consistency a symbol of loving and why does instability produce distance and uninvolvement? Suppose a man thinks he *should* keep up and provide for his family, but in fact has an irregular work history, which he justifies by a string of excuses. He not only detracts from his marriage by earning inadequate income, but he loses self-esteem because he fails to perform consistently with his own standards. And love does not thrive under conditions of low self-esteem. Contrast this with a woman who believes she should not display vehement, abusive anger toward her mate. Most of the time, regardless of situation, she lives within this limit, and when she does so she is confident and assured. In the context of marriage her ability to act within her preferred boundaries symbolizes love, because she offers to her husband a partner whose behavior he can trust and predict.

All of us probably know of at least one case where a husband or wife has failed to maintain self-consistency. Symptoms of this include excessive anger and abuse, irresponsibility in career performance, alcohol abuse, and/or amoral business dealings. In keeping with their chosen behavior, such individuals will often claim that a bad marriage was the cause of their instability. Not only is the claim itself unloving, but it is an evasion of responsibility to blame a marriage for poor individual performance.

Contrast this with what happens when two people chart a course of life in which they remain responsible to themselves and to each other The esteem and self-confidence they feel as a result enables them to logically conclude that the marriage helps rather than hinders, supports rather than detracts. Because they see the rewards their behavior brings, they have the capacity to renew themselves and their marriage. Each person directs his or her actions in ways that are beneficial to both. The couple find their dialogue of marriage one to which they are fully committed, for they have made it a source of continual interest and growth.

BIBLIOGRAPHY

BACH, G. R., and P. WIDEN, *The Intimate Enemy*. New York: Morrow, 1969.

BATESON, G., *Steps to an Ecology of Mind*. New York: Ballantine Books, 1972.

BIRDWHISTELL, R., *Kinesics and Context*. Philadelphia: University of Pennsylvania Press, 1970.

BUBER, M., *Knowledge of Man*. New York: Harper and Row, 1965.

CAIRNS, R. B., The informational properties of verbal and non-verbal events. *Journal of Social Psychology* 5 (1967), 353–357.

CLEVELAND, E. J., and W. D. LONGAKER, Neurotic patterns in the family, in *The Psycho-Social Interior of the Family* (ed. by Gerald Handel). Chicago: Aldine, 1967.

COLLINS, B. E., and H. GUETZKOW, *A Social Psychology of Group Processes for Decision Making*. New York: Wiley, 1964.

CULBERT, S. A., *The Interpersonal Process of Self-Disclosure: It Takes Two to See One*. New York: Renaissance Editions, 1968.

HOMANS, G., Social behavior as exchange, in *Current Perspectives in*

Social Psychology (ed. by E. P. Hollander and R. G. Hunt). Toronto, Oxford University Press, 1967.

JOURARD, S. M., *The Transparent Self.* Princeton University Press, Princeton, N.J., 1964.

KANTOR, D., and W. LEHR, *Inside the Family.* Washington: Jossey-Bass, 1975.

KATZ, M., Agreement on connotative meaning in marriage. *Family Process* 4 (March 1964), 64–74.

LAING, R. D., H. PHILLIPSON, and A. R. LEE, *Interpersonal Perception.* New York: Harper and Row, 1966.

LEDERER, W., and D. JACKSON, *Mirages of Marriage.* New York: Norton, 1968.

LIDZ, T., *The Origin and Treatment of Schizophrenic Disorders.* New York: Basic Books, 1973.

LOOMIS, J. L., Communication, the development of trust, and cooperative behavior. *Human Relations* 12 (1959), 305–315.

MASLOW, A., Holistic-dynamic theory, in *Theories of Personality* (ed. by Calvin S. Hall and Gardner Lindzey). New York: Wiley, 1957.

MASTERS, W. H., and V. JOHNSON, *The Pleasure Bond.* Boston: Little, Brown, 1975.

MOULTON, J. S., and R. R. BLAKE, *The Marriage Grid.* New York: McGraw-Hill, 1971.

MERHABIAN, A., *Silent Messages.* Belmont, Calif.: Wadsworth, 1971.

PERLS, F. S., *Gestalt Theory Verbatim.* Lafayette, Calif.: Real People Press, 1969.

PRUITT, D. G., and J. L. DREWS, The effect of time pressure, time elapsed, and the opponent's concession rate on behavior in negotiation. *Journal of Experimental Social Psychology* 5 (1969), 43–60.

RADLOW, R., and M. F. WEIDNER, Unenforced commitments in "cooperative" and "non-cooperative" non-constant-sum games. *Journal of Conflict Resolution* 10 (1966), 497–505.

ROTTER, J. B., Generalized expectancies for internal versus external control of reinforcement. *Psychological Monographs* 80 (1966), 1–28.

RUBIN, J. Z., and B. R. BROWN, *The Social Psychology of Bargaining and Negotiation.* New York: Academic Press, 1975.

SATIR, V., *Conjoint Family Therapy.* Palo Alto, Calif.: Science and Behavior Books, 1967.

THARP, R. G., Psychological patterning in marriage. *Psychological Bulletin* 60, No. 2 (March 1963), 97–117.

WATZLAWICK, P., J. BEAVIN, and D. JACKSON, *Pragmatics of Human Communication.* New York: Norton, 1967.

WINTERS, W. D., and J. FERREIRA, *Research in Family Interaction.* Palo Alto, Calif.: Science and Behavior Books, 1969.

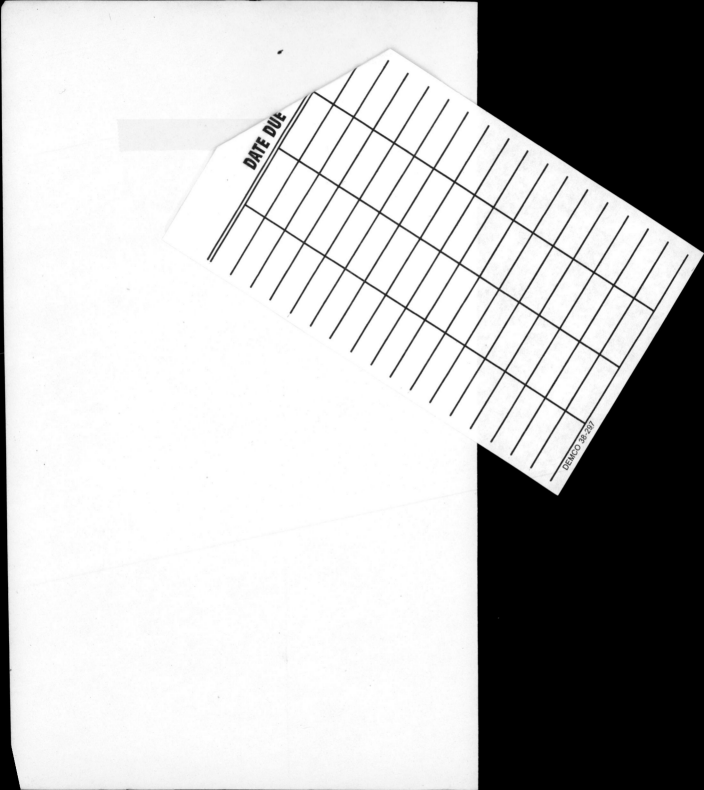

DATE DUE

DEMCO 38-297